1006873341

MODERN WORLD NATIONS

Egypt

Second Edition

Joseph J. Hobbs
University of Missouri–Columbia
with additional text by Aswin Subanthore

Series Editor
Charles F. Gritzner
South Dakota State University

CHELSEA HOUSE
PUBLISHERS
An imprint of Infobase Publishing

Frontispiece: Flag of Egypt

Cover: The Nile River at Aswan, Egypt.

Egypt, Second Edition

Copyright © 2007 by Infobase Publishing

Chelsea House
An imprint of Infobase Publishing
132 West 31st Street
New York NY 10001

Library of Congress Cataloging-in-Publication Data
Hobbs, Joseph J. (Joseph John), 1956-
 Egypt / Joseph Hobbs ; with additional text by Aswin Subanthore. — 2nd ed.
    p. cm. — (Modern world nations)
 Includes bibliographical references and index.
 ISBN-13: 978-0-7910-9515-7 (hardcover)
 ISBN-10: 0-7910-9515-0 (hardcover)
 1. Egypt—Juvenile literature.   I. Subanthore, Aswin.   II. Title.   III. Series.

 DT49.H63 2007
 962—dc22

2007010466

Chelsea House books are available at special discounts when purchased in bulk quantities for businesses, associations, institutions, or sales promotions. Please call our Special Sales Department in New York at (212) 967-8800 or (800) 322-8755.

You can find Chelsea House on the World Wide Web at http://www.chelseahouse.com

Series design by Takeshi Takahashi
Cover design by Joo Young An

Printed in the United States of America

Bang NMSG 10 9 8 7 6 5 4 3 2 1

This book is printed on acid-free paper.

All links and Web addresses were checked and verified to be correct at the time of publication. Because of the dynamic nature of the Web, some addresses and links may have changed since publication and may no longer be valid.

Table of Contents

Egypt

Second Edition

CHAPTER

1

Introducing Egypt

O n September 11, 2001, two large passenger jets flew into the World Trade Center towers in New York City, and a third plane struck the Pentagon in Washington, D.C. Within days, U.S. intelligence sources traced the attacks and another that caused the crash of a plane in rural Pennsylvania to al-Qaeda, an organization financed by a Saudi Arabian named Osama bin Laden. But bin Laden's right-hand man, the one believed to be responsible for planning the attack, was an Egyptian. Some of the hijackers of the planes were Egyptian. As American planes began bombing targets associated with Osama bin Laden in Afghanistan, some Egyptians took to the streets of Cairo in protest against the United States. Egypt seemed to be living up to its reputation as a hotbed of Islamic unrest and a breeding ground for terrorism.

That is the Egypt in the news during recent years. But open up a *National Geographic* magazine, a coffee-table book about the wonders of the world, or a book on Western civilization, and a different Egypt can be seen. It is a land of temples and tombs, of pharaohs and pyramids, of camels and sand. It is a photogenic and mysterious land, so unlike the United States, yet somehow linked to the American way of life—it is the birthplace of paper and written language, of monumental architecture, and of irrigation.

There is an Egypt many in the United States have probably not seen, the homeland to more than 80 million generous, gregarious, and proud people who today call themselves Egyptians. They are Muslim and Christian, city dwellers and village peasants, globally involved businesspeople and remote desert nomads. Some are wealthy, but most are not. Nearly all of them, though, have one custom in common: If they were to see a stranger passing by their home, they would cry out, "*Ahlan wa sahlan*"—"welcome!" and beckon that person to come meet them and enjoy their hospitality.

How can people understand these different Egypts? How can a culture of hospitality and generosity produce people who also hate and destroy? How can so much have been accomplished so long ago in a country that is almost completely barren desert? And what does the West owe to that ancient culture? By answering these and other questions, this book will introduce the extraordinary country that is Egypt.

Look at Egypt—officially known as the Arab Republic of Egypt—on a world map. One obvious feature is the country's central location relative to the continents of Africa, Asia, and Europe. If the Middle East is the crossroads of the three continents, then Egypt is the crossroads of those crossroads. In the very distant past, the earliest humans came out of Africa to populate Asia and Europe. They would have passed through Egypt. People, and cultures bearing their ideas, and materials, have crisscrossed Egypt for thousands of years, leaving their mark on the country's land and life. In return, many borrowed Egyptian cultural elements. Egypt continues to be an important crossroads even today. By sea, the shortest distance

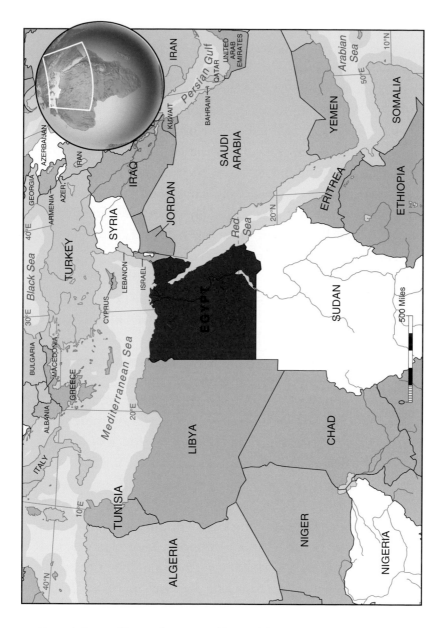

Egypt is located in northeastern Africa and borders three countries: Libya to the west, Sudan to the south, and Israel to the northeast. Egypt is slightly more than three times the size of the state of New Mexico and is the thirtieth-largest country in the world.

between Europe and the Far East is through the Mediterranean Sea, the Suez Canal, and the Red Sea—through Egypt. Egypt's Suez Canal, opened in 1869, is one of the world's most important waterways. Keeping it open to international sea traffic is essential to the economic well-being of many countries.

Look closely at the map again. Notice that Egypt occupies portions of two continents. In the extreme northeast is the triangular peninsula called Sinai, which sits in Asia. The Suez Canal marks the dividing line between Asia and Africa. Leaving Sinai—Asia, that is—one can actually drive through a tunnel beneath the canal and emerge a few seconds later in Africa. That is where most of Egypt is located.

Driving westward from the Suez Canal, one would cross mostly flat, open desert country for about two hours. This is the Eastern Desert. There are no villages or towns, only a few bus stops and coffee shops. Then the landscape begins to change. Factories first, then some apartment blocks, and ever more traffic, and in the sky above looms a seemingly ever-present brownish haze. Soon there are high-rise buildings standing side by side, and traffic comes to a crawl. Welcome to Cairo! With perhaps as many as 20 million people living in its metropolitan area, Cairo is the largest city in Africa and the Middle East. This area is also the Nile Valley. The drive from the eastern outskirts of Cairo to its downtown on the banks of the Nile takes less than an hour. Cairo is the heart of Egypt—the great city Egyptians call *Umm ad-Dunya*, "the Mother of the World."

Nearly 2,500 years ago, the Greek historian and geographer Herodotus called Egypt "the gift of the Nile." The river has always been Egypt's lifeblood, and Egypt probably would be no more world famous than, say, Chad or Paraguay if the Nile did not run through the country. Egypt without the Nile would also be a country with few people. The Nile has deposited some of the world's best agricultural soils along its floodplain, and for thousands of years Egypt has been a prolific producer of

The city of Aswan, located in Upper Egypt, is the southern terminus of the Nile River valley. Below Aswan, the Nile flows through several cataracts and dams and the region is extremely dry. Pictured here is the Old Cataract Hotel, with the Nile River to the left.

cereal crops, fruits, and vegetables. Until quite recently, Egypt was able to produce more than enough food for the people living on the shores of the Nile. And even today, this is where 9 out of every 10 Egyptians live. A map showing the population distribution in Egypt is astonishing—the dots representing thousands of people create a perfect outline map of the Nile River and the Nile Delta on the Mediterranean, and there are few dots elsewhere.

Driving north from Cairo, there are lush cotton fields and numerous cities and villages along the delta. From Cairo, it is possible to reach the Mediterranean Sea in about four hours. The roads stretching southward along the Nile pass through bright green fields and innumerable settlements, mostly villages—southern Egypt is more rural and poorer than the north. After a three-day trip, the Nile Valley stops at the frontier city of Aswan. It has a distinctively African feeling, and while the weather in the previous places you visited was warm, it is now hot. The Nubian people who live here are darker skinned than the Egyptians downstream (to the *north*), and many goods in Aswan's markets are from sub-Saharan Africa. South of town there is a giant dam that blocks the Nile River, and stretching southward from the dam all the way into neighboring Sudan is a great reservoir, Lake Nasser.

West of the Nile Valley, paralleling its entire course through Egypt, is another desert, even more arid and forbidding than the one between the Suez Canal and Cairo. It is the Western Desert. There are a few oases, green islands of date palms rising from a desert sea, where people do live, but except for these and a thin line of settlements along the Mediterranean coast, the Western Desert is a vast and largely uninhabited wilderness stretching from the Nile to Libya.

Egypt is thus a geographically "simple" country: A densely populated river valley cuts through almost unpopulated deserts. In political and cultural terms, Egypt is richer and more complex. To appreciate its place in the world, it is necessary to begin by recognizing that its population is quite large for a country its size (deserts included). Egypt's 80 million people make up almost a quarter of the population of the Middle East. Just in demographic terms, then, Egypt carries a lot of importance in the region and offers a good pulse of the body that is the Middle East. The country is the cultural capital of the Middle East. In the region, Cairo is like Hollywood and Nashville combined, producing films and music that audiences across the

Arabic-speaking world devour. Predominately Muslim, Egypt also is a source of Islamic scholarship and civilization. When leading Egyptian clerics speak on important issues, their words travel as far west as Morocco and east to Indonesia.

Egypt's influence in international political affairs is also strong. Egypt was the first Arab country to make peace with Israel, the longtime adversary of the Arab world. It was a risky move. In signing a peace treaty, Egypt earned the status it retains today as a reasonable, moderate, reliable country; a friend of the West in a region where many countries are known for radicalism, strife, and anti-Western sentiment. But the peace treaty also angered many within Egypt and throughout the Middle East who believed that Arabs should never make peace with Israel. As the United States rewarded Egypt for making peace with Israel with large amounts of economic aid, and gradually placed more and more soldiers and military assets in the region, much of the growing anger was also directed against the United States. And then came September 11.

It is time to explore Egypt, this land of war and peace, river and desert, Islam and Christianity, antiquity and modernity. Travel through its natural landscapes, survey its rich history, and see how Egyptians live and how they view the world. Find out why the country is struggling economically and wrestling with political problems. Finally, look to the future of this "antique land," as the British poet Shelley called Egypt.

2

Physical Landscapes

Most of Egypt is situated in the northeastern corner of Africa, but Egypt also includes southwest Asia's Sinai Peninsula. The country extends about 1,170 miles (1,883 kilometers) south to north, from about 22 to 32 degrees north latitude—so, only southernmost Egypt lies in the tropics. It also spans a distance of 760 miles (1,223 kilometers) west to east, from about 25 to 35 degrees east longitude. Egypt's total area is 386,662 square miles (1,001,450 square kilometers), or an area about the combined size of Texas, Oklahoma, and New Mexico. Egypt's neighbors are Libya to the west, Israel to the northeast, and Sudan to the south. The northern border is formed by the Mediterranean Sea, while the Gulf of Suez and Red Sea make up the eastern border of mainland Egypt. The Sinai Peninsula forms a narrow wedge between Africa and Asia and is framed by the Mediterranean Sea on the north, the Isthmus of

Suez and Gulf of Suez on the west, and the Gulf of Aqaba and Israeli border on the east.

WEATHER AND CLIMATE

Egypt has a hot desert climate. Because the country is in the lower middle latitudes of the Northern Hemisphere, the highest temperatures are in the summer months of June through August, and the coldest period is December through February. From north to south across Egypt, there are three climatic zones. The Mediterranean coast belt gets between three and eight inches (76 to 203 millimeters) of rain each year and has a January average low temperature of 48°F (9°C) and an average July maximum temperature of 86°F (30°C). The Middle Egypt belt (southward to about 29 degrees north latitude) gets only up to about 1½ inches (38 millimeters) of rain yearly (in Cairo) and has only slightly higher temperatures than the Mediterranean zone. The Upper (to the south, from which the Nile flows) Egypt belt, where rainfall is scarce indeed, typically gets between no rainfall to one-tenth of an inch (three millimeters) per year. People living anywhere in the eastern two-thirds of the United States get far more rain from a single thunderstorm than southern (Upper) Egypt will get in 10 years. It is hot there, too: At the southern Nile city of Aswan, the average July high is a torrid 108°F (42°C). However, winter nights can also be cool: The average low temperature in January is 49°F (9.3°C). During the season the Egyptians call *khamsin* (meaning 50 days), from March through May, hot Saharan winds cause sandstorms across the country, making even northern cities like Cairo feel Aswan-like for a few days.

These are the broad features of Egypt's climate, but local conditions vary a good deal where there are mountains, especially in the Sinai Peninsula and in easternmost mainland Egypt. Temperatures decrease with elevation and can be determined by using a simple formula: 3.6°F (2°C) per 1,000 feet (305 meters). The mountains tend to "make" rain, too—an effect geographers

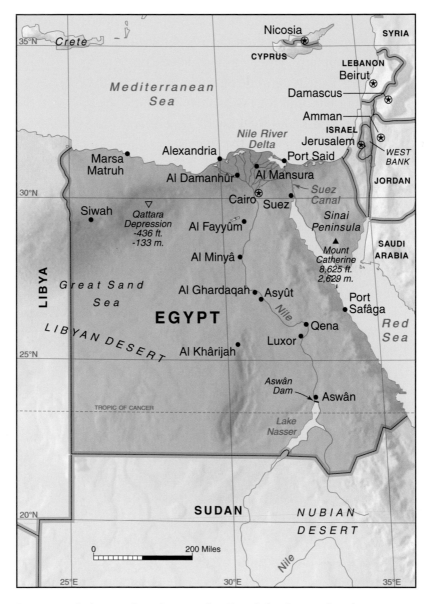

Deserts and plateaus largely comprise Egypt's landscape, but the area around the Nile River and delta is fertile and thus home to the majority of the country's population. The Nile River also divides the Eastern and Western deserts, each of which has distinct characteristics: The Eastern Desert is dissected by wadis (dry beds of seasonal rivers) and is bordered on the east by mountains, whereas the Western Desert is extremely arid and is devoid of wadis.

call orographic precipitation—so Egypt's highlands are wetter and have more vegetation than lower regions. Still, these are desert mountains, and Egypt is a desert country.

Egypt's main natural landscape regions are the Nile Valley, the Nile Delta, and the Suez Canal Zone; the North Coast, the Western Desert, and the Eastern Desert; and the Sinai Peninsula. The following journey will illustrate how people who have occupied Egypt for a very long time have used and changed these landscapes.

THE NILE VALLEY, THE NILE DELTA, AND THE SUEZ CANAL ZONE

Within the desert that is Egypt, the Nile Valley is a long, thin oasis. While the deserts, which the ancients called the Red Land, make up about 96 percent of the country, human life in Egypt has always been focused on the fertile Black Land along the river. Despite its vast wilderness, Egypt is synonymous with civilization; its Arabic name, *Masr*, comes from the verb meaning "to found, build, settle, civilize, colonize." And that civilization is synonymous with the Nile.

The Nile River has two sources, one in highland Ethiopia at Lake Tana, which feeds the Blue Nile, and the other in Central Africa around Lake Victoria, which feeds the White Nile. At their junction at Khartoum, Sudan, the Blue Nile accounts for about 70 percent of the river's summer high-season volume. Until contained by two twentieth-century dams at Aswan, the surge of summer rainwater from the fertile Ethiopian highlands inundated much of Egypt's Nile floodplain every August through September. Each flood left a deposit of about 1/20 of an inch (1 millimeter) of silt yearly, building very fertile sediments that are now about 25 feet (8 meters) deep.

Nearly all of Egypt's farmland is found in that 14,000-square-mile (36,260-square-kilometer) "river oasis" consisting of the Nile Valley, known traditionally as Upper Egypt, and the Nile Delta, known as Lower Egypt. The Nile runs almost due north, so in Egypt it is necessary to switch the usual orientation and think of south as "up" and north as "down." The green ribbon of the Nile Valley is narrow, only about 6 miles (10 kilometers) wide on average. Escarpments, or cliffs, of sandstone and limestone up to 1,000 feet high (305 meters) trace long stretches of the valley's desert borders. There is a break in this cliff wall southwest of Cairo, where a canal carries Nile water into a fertile depression called the Faiyum.

Transformation of the Egyptian Nile from a natural to a cultural landscape has been occurring for more than 7,000 years. Around 5000 B.C., Neolithic people in the Faiyum saw perhaps half the river's floodplain covered with savanna grasses and dry thickets. In these habitats the people grazed domestic sheep, goats, pigs, and cattle, and hunted elephant and hartebeest (African antelope). From the river, they took Nile perch and other fish, trapped birds, and hunted hippopotamus and crocodile. They grew barley and emmer wheat, planting their crops after the annual floodwaters retreated in late October. They left the land fallow after the May harvest—the Nile was far down in its channel, and it was difficult to lift up enough water to plant a second summer crop.

With some improvements, this simple technology of seasonal flood irrigation sustained the civilization of Pharaonic Egypt (3100–332 B.C.). The conversion to permanent, or perennial, irrigation began modestly around 1500 B.C. with the introduction of the *shaduf*, a device for lifting water to summer crops. It brought increasing amounts of floodplain wildlands into cultivation. The pace of change quickened under Greek and Roman rule (332 B.C. to A.D. 324). Unused regions of Upper Egypt and the Faiyum were settled and planted with wheat, barley, broad beans, millet, sesame, lentils, clover, and flax. Other water-lifting devices, like the Archimedean screw and waterwheel, were used to irrigate more land along the Nile and its canals. The limit of cultivation set by available technology was almost reached, with the planted area being almost equal to what was planted 2,000 years later, in 1880. Agricultural improvements were accompanied by population growth, with the number of Egyptians doubling in 300 years to almost 5 million in A.D. 50.

The large-scale change from basin to perennial irrigation began in modern times after 1800, with the building of barrages. These low barriers across the Nile lifted water for movement through canals to irrigate summer crops downstream. Then, in 1902, a dam was built to actually store water for use in the summer. This was the low dam placed at Aswan, in southern Egypt. The final conversion to perennial irrigation came with construction of the Aswan High Dam, completed in 1970.

Upstream from the Aswan High Dam, a reservoir called Lake Nasser stretches 295 miles (475 kilometers) south to Sudan. As it formed, this lake flooded a region known historically as Nubia. Except for some of the larger and more famous structures that were relocated on higher ground, many ancient Egyptian monuments were lost beneath the rising waters. Nubians, the people who lived along the river, had to be relocated to new settlements. Some of them have since returned to the shores of Lake Nasser to fish and farm, although they must often compete with crocodiles.

The Nile Delta fans out below Cairo, where the river divides into two branches or distributaries, the Rosetta and Damietta, named for the two towns situated at their respective mouths. The delta forms a rough triangle with a north-south span of 100 miles (161 kilometers) from its 130-mile- (210-kilometer-) long base on the Mediterranean to its apex near Cairo. Its area is 8,800 square miles (22,792 square kilometers) (compared with the Nile Valley's 5,200 square miles, or 13,468 square kilometers), or 63 percent of Egypt's inhabited terrain. Along the delta coast is a chain of elongated lakes, from west to east: Maryut, Idku, Burullus, and Manzala. These are brackish (slightly salty) and shallow bodies of water, generally less than three feet (one meter) deep, joined directly to the sea by narrow channels through sandbars and limestone ridges.

As many as seven Nile distributaries once snaked across the delta to create a network of river arms, islands, seasonally flooded basins, and swamps. Around 5000 B.C., Neolithic people exploited the Nile Delta, much as they did the Nile Valley, planting crops, herding animals, and fishing and fowling in the wetlands. During early Pharaonic times (about 2700–2300 B.C.), ancient Egyptians called the wetlands the "bird tanks of pleasure" and the "papyrus lands." Wealthy men hunted birds for sport in these areas, where papyrus and lotus were the most commonly found plants.

People eventually tamed the delta wildlands, although later than the Nile Valley. Beginning around 300 B.C., Greek and later Roman colonists developed the region, turning marshes into vineyards and orchards, and establishing new towns. Pressure on the wetlands intensified. Eventually even papyrus, the Pharaonic symbol of Lower Egypt, became extinct there. The demand for paper products had resulted in its extensive cultivation, although it also grew wild. But the plant was doomed once linen paper was substituted for papyrus in the tenth century. Papyrus was uprooted to make way for new agricultural land. It was gone by 1821.

Nearly adjoining the eastern delta is the Suez Canal Zone. An almost continuous strip of green land borders the 101-mile (163-kilometer) canal between the cities of Port Said on the Mediterranean Sea and Suez on the Gulf of Suez. The canal itself is made up of artificial excavations in sandy plains and of the natural bodies of Lake Timsah and the Great and Little Bitter Lakes. Another important city in the canal zone is Ismailiya, known as Egypt's garden city.

Ever since the canal was completed, there has been an open exchange of marine life between the Red Sea and the Mediterranean. Before the canal was completed in 1869, animals migrated back and forth across the Isthmus of Suez. By this means, for example, the flightless ostrich reached Asia from Africa. Most large mammals found east of the Nile in Egypt are also found in southwest Asia. The canal today is probably making such wildlife exchanges more difficult.

Because of intense human activity on the landscape, the wildlife of the Nile Valley, the Nile Delta, and the Suez Canal

The Suez Canal connects Port Said on the Mediterranean Sea with the town of Suez on the Red Sea. The 101-mile- (163-kilometer-) long canal is twice the length of the Panama Canal and allows goods to be transported from Asia to Europe without having to circumnavigate Africa.

Zone today is not very diverse. Migratory birds are trapped in vast numbers during the autumn for sale as food items. The main mammals are those that farmers have accepted as neighbors and those best at avoiding contact with people: hedgehog, shrew, jackal, fox, mongoose, jungle cat, and wild cat. Domesticated animals have largely taken the place of the large wild animals. Rural people of the Nile Valley and Delta region share their land with cattle, water buffalo, camels, donkeys, sheep, and goats. The pesticides they use to prevent damage to their crops have eliminated some birds of prey and other predators, allowing rats to grow in number. There are very few wild plants and trees. Trees grow mainly on the margins of fields, canals, and roads and include the native date palm and tamarisk, and the introduced Australian pine.

DESERT REGIONS

Egypt's deserts—the Western Desert, the Eastern Desert, and the Sinai—make up most of the country's area and were not always as dry as they are today. The Neolithic period, from 8000 to 3000 B.C., was generally a time of more rains. As much as 4 to 12 inches (100 to 300 millimeters) fell each year west of the Nile, creating semiarid shrub habitats similar to those found in tropical northeast Africa today. During that time, people probably kept cattle and grew crops on what is now completely barren land. They also hunted game animals, including the giraffe. East of the Nile, where there were abundant winter rains, hunters pursued elephants and other savanna game animals. But the rainy period ended about 2400 B.C., and Egypt's climate has been extremely dry ever since. The savanna grasses gave way to barren land. Animals that required a good deal of water to survive became locally extinct. Some people retreated to places of permanent water in the Western Desert oases and along the Nile. Others adjusted to the changing conditions by practicing a pastoral nomadic livelihood (described in Chapter 4), in which they moved with their livestock in search of water and vegetation.

The Western Desert

Sometimes called the Libyan Desert, the Western Desert encompasses 272,400 square miles (705,513 square kilometers), or about two-thirds of Egypt's total area. East to west, it extends from the Nile Valley to the Libyan border, and south to north from the Sudanese border to the Mediterranean Sea. It consists of several plateaus of limestone and sandstone, a vast area of sand, and several depressions that contain oases.

The Western Desert does not have spectacular mountains such as those found in the Sinai Peninsula and Eastern Desert. The highest point is 6,244 feet (1,903 meters) on Jebel Uweinat, a sandstone and igneous range spanning the extreme southwestern corner of Egypt. This is an unusual region in the sterile Western Desert. On average, rain falls once every 7 to 10 years, feeding small springs and supporting plants and animals similar to those found on the other side of the Nile, in the mountainous Eastern Desert. North of Jebel Uweinat is the Gilf Kebir, a divided sandstone plateau rising to 3,300 feet (1,006 meters). The Western Desert's largest natural region is a limestone plateau about 1,650 feet (503 meters) high, rising north of Gilf Kebir and stretching all the way from the Libyan border to the Nile Valley. It is rather lifeless except when rain falls at intervals of only once every 10 years or more, producing patches of "accidental" plant cover.

The Great Sand Sea is a vast body of *erg* (sandy) desert stretching about 480 miles (772 kilometers) north to south from Siwa Oasis to Gilf Kebir, and 120 miles (193 kilometers) west to east from the Libyan border to Farafra Oasis. It consists mainly of almost lifeless sand dunes. People rarely set foot on this desert wilderness, and it has long been a barrier to trade and movement. The Greek geographer and historian Herodotus claimed that 50,000 Persian soldiers died trying to cross it when a ferocious sandstorm overtook them.

Embedded in the Western Desert's limestone plateau are several great oases depressions, the main locations of life in the Western Desert. Their formation began during ancient periods of abundant rainfall, when water widened fractures in the plateau floor. Winds then carved some of these fissures deeper and deeper, finally cutting into water-bearing levels in the limestone rock. This process created the principal oases and depressions of the Western Desert: Wadi el Natrun, Siwa Oasis, Qattara Depression, Bahariya Oasis, Farafra Oasis, and Dakhla Oasis. The typical Western Desert depression is nearly or completely encircled by steep cliffs, or escarpments. Its floor is near or below sea level. There are some good soils, and where water breaks the surface as springs there is a productive irrigated agriculture. In poorly drained low-lying areas of the depression floors, excess water accumulates in salty lakes surrounded by salt marshes, making it impossible to farm. Aside

The Western Desert, also known as the Libyan Desert, is the northeastern arm of the Sahara Desert and extends west from the Nile River into Libya. Encompassing more than 272,000 square miles (704,477 square kilometers), the Western Desert stretches across more than two-thirds of Egypt.

from the oases depressions, the only agriculturally productive area of the Western Desert is its narrow coastal zone along the Mediterranean Sea. There, in a strip about 20 miles (32 kilometers) wide paralleling the sea from the Libyan border to Alexandria, relatively good rains support many crops and about half of all the wild plant species that live in Egypt. Wild animals are scarce. The larger ones, such as the cheetah, oryx antelope, addax antelope, and hartebeest, were hunted to local extinction in the twentieth century.

The Eastern Desert

Also known as the Arabian Desert, the Eastern Desert is bounded by the Nile Valley to the west, the Nile Delta and Suez Isthmus to the north, the Gulf of Suez and Red Sea to the east, and the Sudan border to the south. With a total area of 82,900 square miles (214,710 square kilometers), the Eastern Desert occupies about 21 percent of Egypt's total area, but an area only about one-third that of the vast Western Desert. The region is made up of the Red Sea coastal plain, several limestone and sandstone plateaus, and a north-south range of mountains. Egypt's highest peak (outside the Sinai region), 7,217-foot (2,200-meter) Jebel Shayib al-Banat, crowns the rugged mountain range. In general, the Eastern Desert is very dry, with vegetation cover composed of desert grasses, woody trees, and scrub being limited to the valley floors. But the high mountains intercept moisture, producing a more productive set of plant communities in the high elevations and in the larger drainages separating the mountain ranges. Mammals of these mountains and the plateaus to the west include the sand fox, hyena, sand cat, hyrax (which looks like a large rodent, but is related to the elephant), ibex (shrew), Barbary sheep, and dorcas gazelle. Jebel Elba, a mountain in the extreme south near the Sudanese border, gets more rain than anywhere else in the Eastern Desert and has abundant plant and animal life, including ostrich and leopards that sometimes follow rains across the border from the Sudan. Overall, then, while it is a desert wilderness, the Eastern Desert has more water and wildlife resources than the Western Desert (except for the oases). In fact, pastoral nomads (see Chapter 4) are able to make a living here.

The Sinai Peninsula

The Sinai is a triangular-shaped peninsula occupying 24,400 square miles (63,196 square kilometers), with its base along the Mediterranean Sea and its point, Ras Mohamed, jutting into the Red Sea. It is bordered on the west by the Suez Canal and the Gulf of Suez and on the east by the Gulf of Aqaba and Egypt's 120-mile- (193-kilometer-) long political border with Israel. Sinai's Mediterranean coast has shallow lagoons, sand dunes, sandy plains, and salt marshes. The rest of the peninsula is physically an extension of the Eastern Desert, with coastal plains along the gulfs of Suez and Aqaba, a core of high igneous mountains, plateaus of limestone and sandstone, and aprons of gravel plains draining and flanking the highlands. Just off the Gulf of Aqaba shore and at Ras Muhammad are coral reefs that are world famous among divers and snorkelers. Most of these are protected as national parks.

The mountainous interior of south Sinai contains Egypt's highest mountain, Jebel Katarina (8,625 feet, or 2,629 meters), or Mount Catherine. Another prominent peak is Jebel Musa (7,524 feet, or 2,293 meters), widely believed to be the Biblical Mount Sinai. Sinai's alpine topography accounts for relatively high precipitation and a variety of plant and animal life. These mountains sustain about half of Sinai's roughly 1,000 plant species, which, in turn, make up 40 percent of the total flora of Egypt. Many are endemic, meaning they are found nowhere else in the world. Mammals include foxes, gazelles, and hyenas, but leopards were hunted to local extinction in the 1900s. With its more abundant water and vegetation, Sinai has an even larger population of pastoral nomads than does the Eastern Desert. Chapter 4 introduces them and Egypt's other diverse peoples.

3

Egypt
Through Time

E gypt had one of the world's earliest civilizations, a way of life centered on cities. Archaeologists are still in the process of learning exactly how and why Egyptians made the transition from being nomadic hunters and gatherers to simple farmers and then culturally diverse inhabitants of cities. It is certain that the productivity of early agriculture along the Nile played an important role in this transformation. Increasing output of food crops allowed more people to be fed. Then a growing population was able to find new ways to make agriculture more productive. Social scientists believe that there was also a relationship between agriculture and politics in ancient Egypt. A stratified, ranked society developed under the leadership of strong regional authorities. These leaders determined how and where irrigation canals should be dug, what crops should be planted, and how harvested crops should be distributed.

UPPER AND LOWER EGYPT

At the dawn of recorded history in Egypt, around 3200 B.C., there were really two Egypts under the control of men who made these kinds of decisions: Lower Egypt (the Nile Delta), with a king seated at the chief city of Buto, and Upper Egypt (the Nile Valley), with its king at Nekhen. Egyptian historians have found that the two kingdoms were united for the first time around 3100 B.C. by a warrior king named Menes (or Narmer). For almost the next 3,000 years the Egyptian king, called *pharaoh*, was depicted wearing the "double crown" of Upper and Lower Egypt. There are many other symbols of Egypt's unity, including the papyrus plant of Lower Egypt and the lotus plant of Upper Egypt, and the cobra of Lower Egypt and the vulture of Upper Egypt.

In about 280 B.C., an Egyptian historian named Manetho documented the ancient Egyptian chronology that is still used today. He divided the historical periods into the Old Kingdom (which modern historians date from 2700 to 2200 B.C.), the Middle Kingdom (2050–1800 B.C.), and the New Kingdom (1570–1090 B.C.). Between the Old and Middle Kingdom came the First Intermediate period, and between the Middle Kingdom and New Kingdom came the Second Intermediate period. Manetho identified 30 royal family lines, or dynasties, that ruled during these times; the New Kingdom, for example, was the time of the Eighteenth, Nineteenth, and Twentieth dynasties.

THE OLD KINGDOM

During the Old Kingdom (the Third through Sixth dynasties), the pharaoh ruled the two regions from Memphis, a city located near modern Cairo. He enjoyed more power in this period than in any other time of Egyptian history. Not only was he their supreme leader, but Egyptians also considered him to be a living god. Ancient Egyptian religion was very complex and included numerous gods, but the highest-ranking ones

The Great Sphinx of Giza was built in the third millennium B.C., during the Old Kingdom. Located on the west bank of the Nile River, near present-day Cairo, the 240-foot-long, 66-foot-high statue is made of limestone and has the facial features of a man and the body of a lion.

included the sun-god Ra and the pharaoh, and these two were often merged into a single supreme deity. During the peaceful, prosperous days of the Old Kingdom, Egypt's peasant farmers worked the land from the end of the flood season in October until the April harvest. A great many of them spent the other half of the year working in giant public works projects, including not only canals, but also monuments such as the pyramids. Contrary to many widely held theories, the fundamental purpose of the pyramid was to serve as the pharaoh's tomb. Nearby were the much smaller tombs, called *mastabas*, of the lesser royal family members and the wealthy noblemen who served the king. One of Egypt's richest archaeological sites is the Memphis cemetery of Saqqara, not far from the major pyramids at Giza, where the nobles of the Sixth Dynasty were buried. From decorations inside their mastabas, we can learn much about the daily life and the natural history of ancient Egypt. We see men fishing and catching birds in the marshes, and others hunting antelopes in the desert. They also show women dancing, children playing with pets, people mourning at funerals, craftsmen making jewelry and pottery, and farmers harvesting barley.

THE NEW KINGDOM

The tranquility of the Old Kingdom was followed by civil conflict, droughts, and perhaps even famine during the First Intermediate period. But order was restored during the Middle Kingdom, when many of Egypt's accomplishments were focused on Middle Egypt, or the central part of the Nile Valley between modern Minya and Asyut. Disorder followed in the Second Intermediate period as Egypt was invaded by the Hyksos, people from what is now Syria. The first pharaoh of the New Kingdom expelled these foreigners and prosperity returned to Egypt. Its rulers eventually were able to build an empire that extended as far east as Iraq. Foreign lands ruled by Egypt had to pay the Egyptians tribute, which is a kind of tax in the form of foods, minerals, and other commodities. Much of the wealth was funneled into the hands of a class of priests who, along with the pharaoh, effectively controlled the empire from the Upper Egyptian city of Thebes (modern Luxor).

Egypt's most colorful and controversial king was named Amenhotep IV (1369–1353 B.C.). Like his predecessors, he began his rule from Thebes. But he resented the power of the priests, and he rejected the supremacy of their chief god, a regional deity named Amon. Amenhotep IV, who took his name from that god, then made a complete break with Amon

One of the New Kingdom's most renowned pharaohs was Ramses II (the Great), who built the temple of Abu Simbel between 1290 and 1224 B.C. The temple was located south of Aswan, near the border with Sudan, but was relocated to higher ground in the mid-1960s, when the Aswan High Dam formed Lake Nasser.

and the Theban priests. He insisted there was only one god, the sun-god Aten. He renamed himself Akhenaten after that god and moved Egypt's capital to an obscure place in Middle Egypt. Akhenaten fostered a new, more informal style of art and apparently of human relationships, too. In contrast to the stiff, formal, and heroic portrayal of most kings, he had himself depicted as a rather paunchy, unattractive man, but a caring person who loved his wife (the famous Nefertiti) and children dearly.

Such tender scenes of royal family life also may be seen in the artifacts recovered from the tomb of Egypt's most famous king, Tutankhamen, who was probably the son of Akhenaten. "Tut" was a minor figure who assumed the throne as a boy after Akhenaten's death. The real power behind the throne was with the priests and the military, who returned Egypt's capital to Thebes. Tutankhamen died there and was buried in a tiny tomb that was soon forgotten. It was his obscurity that secured Tutankhamen's ultimate fame, for all of the other, much larger, royal tombs in the Valley of Kings were robbed in ancient times, while Tut's remained sealed for more than 3,000 years. Only in 1922 did English archaeologist Howard Carter breach the tomb's entrance and thrust in a candle to behold what he called "wonderful things."

Another of the New Kingdom's most famous pharaohs was Ramses II (Ramses the Great), who built colossal monuments to himself throughout the land (including Abu Simbel in Nubia) and waged wars against Egypt's Asian enemies. Egypt reached its peak of power in the "Ramesside" times of Ramses II and his immediate successors. Then the sun began to set on the glories of ancient Egypt.

FOREIGN INFLUENCES

During what is known as the Late Dynastic period (1090–332 B.C.), invaders came from Libya, Sudan, Ethiopia, Assyria (modern Iraq), and Persia (modern Iran). The brilliant young Macedonian Greek king, Alexander the Great, conquered Egypt in 332 B.C., beginning the era of Greek control known as the Ptolemaic period. The Ptolemaic rulers saw themselves as sympathetic benefactors of the Egyptian people and even merged many Egyptian gods and beliefs with their own. They built the great city of Alexandria, which for a time was the world's leading center of learning and the arts. A great library stood there until it burned down in the first century A.D. The last Ptolemaic ruler was the famous queen Cleopatra (Cleopatra VI). Through her strong will and personal relationships, she was able for three decades to hold off the Romans from their most fervent desire: to conquer and control Egypt. Cleopatra was the last monarch to wear the double crown, and in that sense 3,000 years of ancient Egyptian history ended with her suicide in 30 B.C.

With Cleopatra's death, Egypt became a province of Rome and was ruled from that center of power. In contrast with the Greek Ptolemaic effort to build strong and friendly ties with the Egyptians, the Romans truly subjugated them. Rome saw Egypt as a colony from which it could take what it needed. Above all, Egypt was to serve as the granary of Rome, providing the motherland with cereal crops and other agricultural produce. Roman agents collected the exotic wildlife of Egypt and lands farther south for the arena games held in Rome. Gold and valuable types of building and ornamental stone were mined and quarried in remote locations in the Eastern Desert for use throughout the Roman Empire. The often brutal labor required to harvest these resources was supplied mainly by peasant peoples forced to work by the Romans. This was the so-called corvée system of labor that other later occupiers of Egypt also used. Rome also placed a huge tax burden on the people of Egypt. Not surprisingly, Egyptians came to despise the Roman occupation.

There were also religious conflicts between many Egyptians and their Roman overlords. Christianity came early to Egypt from Palestine and won many converts. For the first three centuries A.D., Christianity was officially rejected by Rome, and at some times Romans carried out vicious persecutions of Christians. Some devout men fled to the desert to pray in isolation and avoid Roman persecution. Among them were St. Paul and

St. Anthony, who lived in caves in the northern Eastern Desert. Word of their spiritual strength in an environment of hardship and isolation inspired other pious men. They took up residence in nearby cells, or caves, and occasionally congregated together. This was the beginning of monasticism, which developed fully in the Nile Valley and Western Desert oases in the centuries that followed.

The Roman emperor Constantine converted to Christianity and declared it the official religion of the Roman Empire in A.D. 312, bringing an end to the persecution of Christians. Constantine moved the capital of his empire from Rome to Byzantium, which was renamed Constantinople (known today as Istanbul, Turkey). His form of Christianity, known as Byzantine and later as Orthodox Christianity, was Egypt's official faith. It was often uncompromising, and it is a sad legacy of that church that it set about defacing and destroying many of the "heathen" monuments of ancient Egypt. There were also differences in religious doctrine between the Byzantine Church and the form of Christianity practiced by most Egyptians. In A.D. 451, there was an official split between the Byzantine Church and the Coptic Orthodox Church, which originated in Egypt. To this day, most Egyptian Christians are Copts, or Coptic Christians. The Greek Orthodox Church—the successor to Byzantine Orthodoxy—also has followers, including the monks of Sinai's Monastery of St. Katherine.

In A.D. 641, a new faith and way of life swept into Egypt from the Arabian Peninsula. This was Islam. Its followers, called Muslims, practiced a religion revealed to their prophet Muhammad just a few decades earlier. This faith is described in the next chapter. The Muslim army easily defeated the Byzantine forces defending Egypt and settled in for a rather peaceful and tolerant administration of the country. The Arabic-speaking Muslims did little to try to convert the local Coptic Christians and allowed them to run most of their own affairs in their own, mainly Greek, languages. Gradually, more and more Egyptians converted to Islam and adopted the Arabic tongue as their own.

For most of the next 200 years, Egypt was a province of the greater Muslim Abbasid caliphate, based in Baghdad (modern Iraq). The *caliphs* taxed, but otherwise neglected, Egypt. They found themselves unable to rule it effectively and appointed control of Egypt and other provinces to Turkish military officers. One of these Turkish generals, Ahmad Ibn Tulun, briefly made Egypt independent of Baghdad around A.D. 870. His successors were not as strong, and Baghdad once again reasserted control. But in A.D. 969, a new Muslim power invaded from the west and took control away from the Abbasids. These were the Fatimids, whose base was in Tunisia. Unlike most Egyptians, they were Shiite rather than Sunni Muslims, believing that the Prophet Muhammad's successors, the caliphs, should have been his blood relatives rather than elected officials. With one notable exception, however, Fatimid rulers were tolerant of the country's Sunni Muslims, as well as its Christians and Jews. Although there had been ancient Egyptian, Roman, and Byzantine settlements in the area, the Fatimids are credited with founding the city of Cairo. Its Arabic name, *al-Qahira*, means the "Victorious City." The Fatimids encouraged and grew wealthy from regional trade, and Egypt again enjoyed prosperity.

The Fatimids were the last Arabs to rule Egypt for almost a thousand years. In 1171, a Kurdish general from Syria named Salah al-Din (or Saladin) brought an end to their rule. He built his own dynasty, called the Ayyubid, and extended his control over Palestine. With Palestine came Jerusalem, and European Christians intent on regaining its holy places waged a war, one of the Crusades, against Saladin. Ayyubid control of Egypt continued until about 1250. By then, the Ayyubids had come to rely for their power on a class of Turkish soldiers called Mamluks. Officially they were slaves, but they had so much power that they killed the last Ayyubid ruler of Egypt and seized control of the country for themselves. They also fought off the crusaders from Palestine and succeeded in capturing Syria. Mamluk sultans ruled Egypt until 1516, and the country might have enjoyed progress and prosperity but for the ravages of the plague (the Black Death) during the mid-fourteenth century.

In 1516, Egypt fell to the Ottoman Turks, who ruled from Istanbul. Their empire included much of the eastern Mediterranean region and the Arabian Peninsula and was too large to be governed effectively by their available manpower. The Ottomans thus chose to incorporate the Mamluks into their administration of Egypt. Ottoman control of Egypt was never really strong, and the Mamluks reasserted themselves in an environment of growing civil conflict. Egypt was a tempting target for another strong invader.

Egypt's modern history effectively began in 1798, when French forces under the leadership of Napoleon Bonaparte occupied the country. This began a period of European colonial influence and rule over Egypt that greatly changed the country's orientation and priorities.

France's main interest was in Egypt's strategic location. At the time, France and Great Britain were enemies, and each was trying to increase its economic and political power at the expense of the other. France saw control over Egypt as a way to intervene in Great Britain's ability to rule supreme over the land and water routes between Europe and India. French forces met only minimal resistance from Egypt's military and settled in for a brief, but influential, three-year occupation of Egypt. Napoleon dispatched a large team of scholars to Egypt to study and record the country's rich archaeological, natural, historical, and living human heritage. These so-called savants produced an extraordinary multivolume document called *Description de l'Egypte*. They began the science of Egyptology, which has since brought so much of Egypt's rich archaeological past to life.

It also was during the French occupation that the Rosetta Stone was discovered in the Nile Delta. The black basalt stone contained a single official document written in three languages, one of which, Greek, was known to the French. (The other two languages were Egyptian scripts, which up until then had not been decipherable.) With the Rosetta Stone, French scholar Jean-François Champollion was able to unlock the mysteries of the ancient language. Suddenly the modern world could make sense of the treasure trove of written documents and stone inscriptions left by the ancients. Another important legacy of the short French occupation of Egypt was the adoption of French as a second language among educated Egyptians. Even today, the most educated Egyptians learn Arabic, English, and French.

British and Ottoman forces drove the French out of Egypt in 1801. For about the next 75 years, Egypt had some degree of independence from outside powers. A strong ruler named Muhammad Ali, while actually a non-Egyptian (Albanian), struggled to distance the country from its Ottoman Turkish orientation. He wanted to make Egypt an important economic and political power in its own right. A cornerstone of his effort was to make Egypt a leading producer of cotton, which was an important global commodity and therefore could help make Egypt wealthy. His agricultural experts and engineers brought Sudanese long staple cotton to Egypt—the same type that is now famous around the world as Egyptian cotton. They began building barrages that would allow this crop to be irrigated in the Nile Delta during the summer.

In the decades following Muhammad Ali's death in 1849, his grandson and successor, Ismail, tried to make Egypt a more industrialized country. For example, Egyptians built paper processing mills, railways, and modern public works. He also worked with French experts to undertake the building of one of the world's most important waterways, the Suez Canal, which opened for traffic in 1869. Unfortunately, Ismail inherited a burden of debt to European lenders that he paid off in large

Construction on the Suez Canal began in 1859, and after 10 years of work, the canal opened for traffic on November 17, 1869. Workers are pictured here standing in the bed of the canal, which mostly passed through sand and alluvium.

part by selling ownership of the Suez Canal to Great Britain and France.

Great Britain established itself as Egypt's colonial ruler in 1882. Egypt assumed the typical colonial role of providing raw materials—particularly cotton—to the mother country, while Great Britain sold finished products back to Egypt. This relationship was more profitable to Great Britain than to Egypt,

and within Egypt there was resentment and sometimes violence against British rule. Great Britain maintained a firm grip
on Egypt during World War I, as it joined France in decisively
defeating the Ottoman Turks, who had sided with Germany
during the war. With the end of the war in 1918 came the
demise of the "Sick Man of Europe," as the Ottoman Empire
was known. Great Britain and France carved up the Ottoman
lands of the Middle East among themselves, with the British
controlling a swath of territory from Egypt through Palestine
(modern Israel) into Iraq.

Great Britain yielded to increasing postwar demands by
Egyptians that they should rule themselves and granted independence to Egypt in 1922. In many ways, however, it was independence in name only, and British influence remained strong
in Egypt for the next three decades. During this time, Egypt
became a monarchy ruled by a pro-European king. The last
king, Farouk, was ousted in a rebellion by army officers in 1952.
That coup d'etat was officially led by a man named Muhammad Neguib, but he was really a figurehead. The power behind
the revolt was concentrated in the hands of a young officer
named Gamal Abdel Nasser.

Nasser came to power officially in 1956, and over a period
of 15 years, he had a powerful impact on Egypt's society and
its place in the world. He directed what many called a "revolution," appealing to the common man by breaking up the large
land holdings of Egypt's wealthy elite and redistributing them
as smaller parcels to peasants. He aspired to be a leader for all
of the Arab countries by spearheading a 1967 military confrontation with their common enemy, Israel. The results were
disastrous for Egypt (as is described in Chapter 5), but he was
successful in wresting the Suez Canal from foreign control.
He situated Egypt firmly in the orbit of the Soviet Union, but
only after trying to steer a course away from loyalty to either of
the great powers. Although he was not always successful in his

efforts, Nasser did instill in Egyptians a new confidence about themselves and a new sense of solidarity and independence.

Anwar Sadat, who became president of Egypt upon Nasser's death in 1971, reversed the country's direction and sought strong ties with the West, especially the United States. He launched a new war against Israel in 1973, this one more successful than the 1967 conflict, but then made Egypt the first Arab country to sign a peace treaty with Israel (see Chapter 5). His assassination in 1981, carried out in protest over that treaty, brought his vice president, Hosni Mubarak, to power. President Mubarak reaffirmed Sadat's strong relationship with the West and expanded Egypt's role as regional peacemaker. He brought Egypt into the third millennium, a time of great challenge for the country and the region.

The longest-tenured Egyptian head of state, Mubarak has enjoyed unprecedented support for most of his term as president. Particularly popular have been his programs that have supported women's rights and allowed a liberalized influx of Western market goods. He has further developed the country's infrastructure, especially in the southern part of the country, where he has built industrial facilities and new communities. In addition, he has been responsible for the construction of bridges across the Nile and several power plants to generate electricity. And there are plans to build a 1,000-megawatt nuclear power plant on the Mediterranean coast at al-Dabaa. Mubarak also has played a key role in strengthening his nation's role in the global economy by using Egypt's prime location—it serves as a gateway between Europe, Africa, and the Middle East—to his advantage.

Mubarak took control of Egypt during turbulent times. In 1981, when he assumed power, Egypt had only recently signed the 1979 Israel-Egypt Peace Treaty, which came on the heels of the Camp David Accords. Not only did he have to manage relations with Israel, Mubarak also had to pacify an Arab world that was increasingly resentful of what it perceived as Egypt's soft stance toward their nemesis. His role in bridging the gap between the Arab world and Israel during the 1980s was crucial, as was his policy of expanding Egypt's role in international politics.

Although he has upheld the peace treaty with Israel, Mubarak has also condemned Israel's role in relation to Palestine. In fact, his more moderate stance with regard to Israel led the Arab League to reinstate Egypt as a member in 1989. (Egypt's membership was suspended following the peace treaty with Israel.) Founded in 1945, the Arab League promotes economic and cultural cooperation among Arab countries and forbids military confrontation between members. One of the league's seven founding members, Egypt has been an important part of the organization. In fact, six of the seven secretary-generals have been Egyptian. After a 10-year hiatus, during which the Arab League was based in Tunis, Tunisia, the league's headquarters returned to Cairo, placing Egypt squarely in the middle of Arab world politics.

In recent years, several issues have tested Egypt's relation with the Arab world and all other global nations. For example, during the 1990 Iraqi invasion of Kuwait, Egypt provided foot soldiers and was among the first to enter Kuwait. In return, the United States and the European Union granted huge monitory benefits to Egypt that helped its economy immensely. President Mubarak's role in helping address the Israeli-Palestinian conflict helped lead to the 1991 Madrid Peace Conference. Hosted by Spain and cosponsored by the United States and the USSR, the conference was an attempt by the international community to initiate peace negotiations between the two sides.

Under Mubarak, Egypt's foreign policy has changed a good deal. Recent Egyptian policies directed toward helping resolve the region's terrorism problem, as well as Mubarak's effort to make the Middle East nuclear free, have been applauded. For example, during President Nasser's tenure as the nation's head of state, he focused on strengthening ties with the Arab world and mobilizing pan-Arabism. President Mubarak, however, has broadened the scope of Egypt's foreign policy by establishing renewed relationships between Egypt and the United States and European countries.

CHAPTER

4

People
and Culture

Although best known for its wealth of famous ancient artifacts, Egypt also is home to a rich contemporary culture. This
chapter will introduce you to the modern people and ways of
life in Egypt.

ETHNIC GROUPS AND LANGUAGE

Egypt is overwhelmingly an Arab country, in the sense that most of
its people speak Arabic as their native language. Arabic originated
in and around the Arabian Peninsula and is in the Semitic family of
languages that includes Hebrew, spoken by Jews in the world today,
and Aramaic, the language used by Jesus. Arabic speakers settled in
Egypt at different times, but one of the most important migrations
was when Muslim Arabs came to Egypt bearing their new faith in
A.D. 641.

Egypt's ethnic population is fairly uniform. The largest group, of course, is the Egyptians, who comprise 98 percent of the nation's population. Other groups include Berbers, Nubians, Greeks, and Armenians. Cultural interaction with Europe and Africa has had a profound impact on Egyptian ethnicity. In the northern coastal towns of Cairo and Alexandria, European influence is widespread. Contact with Greece and Rome, and later France and Great Britain, have made Egypt very cosmopolitan. In the southern part of the country, a large proportion of the population is Nubian. Approximately 75 percent of the Nubian homeland is in Sudan, but many Nubians relocated to southern Egypt—around the Tosha lakes and Lake Nasser region—in search of agricultural lands. Aswan and Abu Simbel, located in the Upper Egypt region, are Nubian settlements.

Another important ethnic group is the Berbers. Western Egypt, especially around the Siwa oasis and the coastal areas west of Alexandria, are key Berber homelands. The Berber people are among the oldest inhabitants of northern Africa. The Berbers speak their own language and most of them originate from the western Sahara, in Algeria and Morocco. Egyptian Berbers, for the most part, have been "Arabized" and integrated into mainstream Egyptian society. They constitute only a very small fraction of the Egyptian population, yet they have preserved their culture for millennia. Prior to the Arab invasion of the seventh century A.D., the Berbers dominated northwestern Africa and still constitute approximately 30 percent of Morocco's population.

RELIGIOUS GROUPS

There are several religious minorities in Egypt, the most important being the Coptic Christians, who make up about 9 percent of the population. But Egypt is overwhelmingly a Muslim country—about 90 percent of Egyptians practice Islam. Many Muslims throughout the world look to Egypt for

More than 90 percent of Egyptians are Muslim and thus mosques are an important part of any town or city's skyline. Pictured here is the Sultan Hassan Mosque, which was completed in 1363 and appears on Egypt's one-hundred-pound note.

religious inspiration and instruction. One of the world's leading centers of Islamic learning is al-Azhar University, formally organized in A.D. 971 by the Fatimids, shortly after they established the city of Cairo. The clerics of al-Azhar are, like most Egyptians, Sunni or orthodox Muslims who practice a "moderate" form of Islam with little concern for politics or revolt. There are, however, more militant Muslims, and their struggle with the government of Egypt is described in the next chapter.

One of the most noticeable Egyptian traits is their devoutness. Every city and large town has a skyline that includes domes and minarets (towers), the characteristic architectural forms of the mosques where Muslims worship. Five times daily, including at dawn, a call to prayer issues forth from the minarets. Muslims may go to the mosque to pray, and most do on Friday, the Muslim holy day, or they may pray in their homes, offices, or along the street. Prayer is one of the five pillars, or requirements, of Islam. The others are the profession of faith, which requires Muslims to recognize that there is only one God, known as *Allah* in Arabic, and that the Prophet Muhammad was God's messenger; to give alms or charity to the poor; to fast (abstain from food and drinks) from dawn to sunset during the month of Ramadan; and if one is physically and financially able, perform the pilgrimage (*hajj*) to the Saudi Arabian city of Mecca.

POPULATION

Besides Islam, another important characteristic of Egyptian society is the social stratification that exists among rural as well as urban Egyptians. This is the *al-khassa al-amma* cultural system. On one hand there is the *khassa*, or the establishment that tries to impose cultural values. On the other hand there is *amma*, which is based on distribution of welfare among the masses and more common among the youth. The khassa system is more prevalent among rural communities, where local administrations and laws are important and often dictate the lives of the common citizen. There exists a constant struggle between the more established and older khassa and the progressive amma ideologies of local people, especially the Westernized youth. Many Egyptians associate this with the legacy of British colonization and close proximity to Europe resulting in a sharp cultural clash between tradition-bound Islamic society and European lifestyles and values. In this regard, Egypt represents an interesting case of a clash of cultural values that is indeed the sign of times to come.

Another feature that might impress a first-time visitor to Egypt is how many Egyptians there are. Egypt is a populous country, among the top three in the Middle East. With its approximately 80 million people, it is rivaled only by Turkey (71 million) and Iran (65 million), within the region. All but about 5 percent of Egyptians live on the narrow ribbon of the Nile Valley and in the Nile Delta, so impressions of overpopulation and crowding are strong.

Until recently, Egypt's population growth was so rapid that it was considered explosive. Many social scientists warned that there was a population "bomb" that would explode in Egypt, resulting in growing poverty, hunger, famine, and epidemic, or even warfare. The population rocketed from 2.5 million in the early 1800s to about 10 million in 1900, 20 million in 1950, 40 million in 1980, and 70 million in 2002. The primary cause of this meteoric growth was a sharp decline in death rates. Fewer children died and people generally lived longer because of better food production and distribution, and because medical care and technologies improved. At the same time, birthrates remained high. Egypt is like most of the world's other developing countries in that parents often believe that having more children will actually help them lead more prosperous lives. For example, more children mean more hands to work in the fields in rural areas, or to work in a clothing factory or an automobile mechanic shop in the cities. There are no laws against child labor in Egypt. This point of view is different from that of most American parents, who are more likely to believe that if they have fewer children the family will be more prosperous.

Around the world, there is clear evidence that the wealthier parents are, and the more education they have, the fewer children they will have. This correlation has been proving true even in Egypt in recent years. Egypt's level of education has risen in the past few decades, and at the same time, the birthrate—a reflection of how many children Egyptians are choosing to have—has been falling. So, while Egypt's population is very large and continues to grow, the rate of growth has slowed. In 1985, the population was growing at an annual rate of 2.7 percent. At that rate, the country's population would have doubled in 27 years. In 2007, though, the population growth rate had dropped to 1.7 percent. If that rate continues, the country's population will be nearly 100 million by 2030. This is an improvement in a relatively poor country with limited agricultural and other resources. But the sheer number of people added to the population every year is of much concern. In 2006, there were nearly 40 million more Egyptians, a staggering 63 percent more, than in 1985.

Another characteristic of Egypt's people is how young they are—how many infants, children, and young adults there are among the population. It is not a mistaken impression. More than one-third—35 percent—of Egyptians are under the age of 15.

Finally, a visitor's impression of Egypt's population might be one of surprise that so many people live in cities—Westerners might have had an image of Egyptians working the land as they did in Biblical times. Recently, however, not only have Egypt's cities grown rapidly, but their proportion in the overall population has also increased. In 2007, nearly half of Egyptians were city dwellers (versus about 20 percent in 1910), so the rural people are only a modest majority.

Egypt's rural peasant farmers, called *fellahin* in Arabic, live in some 4,000 villages in the Nile Valley and Nile Delta. The typical village is a densely packed group of *adobe* (mud brick) structures built in the midst of the green cultivated area. As in ancient times, Egyptian peasants today build their cemeteries on nearby desert margins, or on unproductive land near the village. The quaint images of men and women in flowing robes and children riding donkeys in these villages lead many outsiders to speak of the timeless Egyptian village. But the villages

The typical rural Egyptian dwelling is composed of adobe (mud bricks) and located along the Nile River. Farmers who live in settlements like the one pictured here, near Cairo, rely on the Nile's water to cultivate their crops.

are changing: Electric pumps are replacing human- or animal-powered water-lifting techniques, and paved roads, electricity lines, telephones, and televisions can be found in all but the most remote villages.

What has not changed as much as Egyptians would like is the general poverty of the village. Despite land reform since the time of President Nasser, few peasants own more than very small farm plots. There simply is not enough good farmland in the Nile Valley and Nile Delta to go around for the growing population. Neither is there sufficient nonfarming jobs in the countryside. The result is that people flee the countryside to seek jobs in the cities. Social scientists call them "nonselective migrants," people who have been "pushed" off the land because the land cannot support them. Also leaving the villages and going to the cities are the "selective migrants," the most educated and ambitious villagers, who are "pulled" to the city by the near certainty that they will find productive employment there. In this way, they represent what is called a "brain drain," meaning the rural areas will probably stay underdeveloped in part because the people best able to do something about the poverty are leaving these places. Regardless of the push-and-pull factors that influence their decision to move, in the end they represent more people in the cities. This helps to explain why Egypt has such crowded urban areas.

Cairo

Egypt's largest city by far is Cairo, with a population estimated to be as many as 15 to 20 million in the metropolitan area. It is an urban giant, a megacity, the largest city in Africa and one of the largest in the world. Up to 25 percent of all Egyptians, and half of the country's urban population, live in Cairo. The second-ranking city is Alexandria (about 4 million), along the Mediterranean coast. Other important cities of the Nile Delta are Tanta and al-Mahalla al-Kubra, and major cities of the Nile Valley are Minya, Asyut, Qena, and Aswan.

Cairo has a clear geographic reason for being Egypt's leading city—it is strategically located near the junction of the Nile Delta and the Nile Valley. It is really several cities established one next to another over time, beginning with the ancient Egyptians, and gradually fused into one flowing whole. The historic heart of the city is in the east, where the Fatimids established walled al-Qahira in A.D. 969. It has all the typical elements of the classic Middle Eastern city, known in Arabic as a *medina* (walled for protection). It has monumental places of worship, including many mosques with their distinctive domes and minarets; and it has a sprawling *suq*, or marketplace, clearly recognizable as the forerunner of the modern Western shopping mall. It also has a rather chaotic street plan that was not laid out along the Western grid system and was never designed for modern vehicular traffic. Thus, the old city has had great new swaths cut into it and elevated highways erected above it to accommodate Cairo's infamous traffic.

A walk though Cairo's medina is truly an enchanting, colorful, and noisy stroll through time. It can also be a bit disheartening, because it is one of the poorer parts of the city. Some people, such as shopkeepers, craftsmen, and taxi drivers, have steady but not well-paying work. And there is a large and poor underclass of beggars and street vendors (people who will, for example, approach a rider in a car to sell a flower necklace or a pack of tissues). The wealthier people tend to live farther west in the newer part of the city, or in the suburbs that have cropped up in recent decades on the city's desert edges. Some of these suburbs, such as Zamalek on Gezira Island, are quite affluent. Many diplomats and successful businesspeople live here, and their children attend Egypt's private schools and universities. Their homes and apartments are spacious and well furnished, and they own automobiles. This is in great contrast with the majority of Egyptians, inside and outside the cities, who often live in cramped and deteriorating quarters and could only dream of having cars and other luxuries.

Cairo's most unique area is the so-called City of the Dead, in the eastern part of the city. It began as flat open space well away from the city and was a logical place to have a cemetery. Many of the wealthy Turkish Mamluks were buried here in magnificent mausoleums. Over time, citizens of Cairo established small family burial plots there, and it grew into a sprawling cemetery. The citizenship of the City of the Dead began to

In the eastern part of Cairo lies the City of the Dead. Originally constructed as a burial ground for Cairo's residents, the area has recently become a home for migrants and the city's poor. Unable to find affordable housing, the inhabitants take up residence in mausoleums and crypts.

change dramatically after Egypt's war with Israel in 1973. That war was centered on the Suez Canal Zone, where many civilians chose to flee their homes in the cities of Port Said, Ismailia, and Suez. They sought safety in Cairo, but there was not sufficient housing for them in apartments. These refugees began to settle in places where there were four walls, though seldom with a roof overhead—the walled cemetery compounds of the City of the Dead. In time, some moved into Cairo's apartments, or back to their rebuilt canal cities. But someone new is always arriving in Cairo from some distant town or village, and more people settled in the cemetery. Some eventually put a roof over the compound, then a second story or even a third. Now, while the dead are still buried here, it is mainly a city of the living. Cairo and Egypt's leaders were embarrassed by the impression given of Egyptians forced to live in a graveyard and for a time tried to relocate the inhabitants. But there was not enough money to build new quarters for all these squatters, and the authorities finally relented and began to treat the City of the Dead like any other part of Cairo. Today, it has most of the services found elsewhere in Cairo, including electricity, running water, telephone lines, and mail.

Northeast of the City of the Dead is another of Cairo's unique areas, the quarter of the *zabbaleen*, or trash collectors. They are Coptic Christians who have collected and sorted Cairo's trash for generations. As most Cairenes (residents of Cairo) sleep, the zabbaleen cover almost every nook and cranny of the city collecting the waste in straw baskets. They load the trash onto a donkey-pulled cart in the street and by daybreak return to their base. Here they begin sorting the waste: Paper, plastic, glass, metal, and other materials are separated into various piles, and organic waste is directed to a giant compost heap. Very little of this waste actually ends up as waste. Most of it is recycled so that, for example, you may buy a bag of peanuts in which the bag is a rather clean sheet of paper on which a student did homework a few days earlier. The recycling is profitable for the zabbaleen. Although their part of the city has giant mounds of refuse, the people are not poor, and they have come far with their enterprise. Recently, they won an official contract to collect Cairo's waste, beating bids for more modern, motorized Western-style collection systems. They also won a prestigious United Nations environmental award that recognized the Earth-friendliness of their labors.

To the Westerner accustomed to the potential dangers of urban life, especially violent crime, perhaps the most surprising feature of the Egyptian city is the overwhelming sense of security. Violence is almost unknown, and even petty theft is rare. Sometimes a pickpocket will lift a wallet on an overcrowded bus, but that is about the extent of the city's crime. A foreigner can walk day or night in any part of Cairo, even its poorest quarters, and not fear for his or her safety. More likely than not, the visitor will be greeted repeatedly by the locals: "Hello, where are you from? Come, come, have tea, meet my family." Hospitality and generosity are important traits in Arab culture, and perhaps no Arabs are friendlier than the Egyptians. That tradition of kindness, as well as their deep religious beliefs, probably has a lot to do with Egypt's low crime rate.

The Bedouin

Yet another culture associated with hospitality is found in Egypt, but far from the big cities and the villages of the Nile Valley. In the deserts live the Bedouin, Arabic-speaking pastoral nomads who came to Egypt from the Arabian Peninsula many centuries ago. They keep livestock—animals such as sheep, goats, and camels that feed on pasture—and move about the desert to find places where there has been rain and therefore plants on which the animals can feed. Their way of life is thousands of years old. It emerged in the Middle East not long after people domesticated plants and animals and began farming. The Bedouin livelihood can be difficult. Sometimes there are long droughts that make it difficult to keep livestock healthy. And sleeping out under the stars or in a wool tent, never having a house or a village to call home, can be a challenge. There are none of the modern conveniences of life, and there is no medical care in the wilderness. But the Bedouins pride themselves on the freedom afforded by their migratory way of life. Traditionally, they have not had to pay taxes, to serve in the military, or to perform forced labor like many of their village-dwelling counterparts.

Before the mid-twentieth century, villagers, pastoral nomads, and urbanites were part of a framework of trade relationships that was generally beneficial to all. A geographer called these relationships the "ecological trilogy." The village peasant farmers were the cornerstone of the trilogy. They grew the cereal grains, fruits, and vegetables that fed city people. Desert pastoral nomads also ate farmers' produce, buying flour, for example, when they visited towns periodically to sell their livestock. Villagers benefited in that exchange. Because they often lacked enough land to support animals like sheep and goats, by trading with the Bedouins they could get these animals' meat, hide, horn, milk, wool, and bone. City people, too, gave something back to the villagers in the form of education, trained medical providers and equipment, and entertainment such as music.

These relationships continue, but they are not as clearly defined or recognizable as before. Most of Egypt's Bedouins have now settled down and have effectively dropped out of the trilogy; only in the Eastern Desert are there still traditional nomads. They have chosen to settle, generally because they have been tempted by the more reliable and profitable work available to them as wage laborers. For example, they often find work as mechanics, guards, and guides in desert towns. Most live in fixed dwellings in or near the desert towns. The family still keeps some animals, but usually only a few, rather than the 40 or 50 sheep and goats they used to have in the wilderness.

Even though their ways of life have changed, all of these people still call themselves Bedouin, and they still affiliate with the tribe more than with any other unit. Ma'aza tribespeople, for example, call themselves Ma'aza and do not really think of themselves as Egyptian. To be a member of a tribe means to have descended from a single, common male ancestor who lived many generations ago. A tribal person almost always

Beginning in the 1950s and '60s, many Bedouins decided to settle in towns and cities, rather than continue to lead a nomadic lifestyle. Today, most Bedouins live in fixed dwellings and they no longer solely practice herding.

marries within the tribe—it is frowned upon to do otherwise. In the desert, the tribes have separate areas in which pasture, water sources, and game animals belong to them. Traditionally, one tribe has always shared its resources with others, knowing that it, too, may need to call on others in a time of drought or other environmental stress.

Agricultural Settlement

In recent years, Egypt's agricultural way of life has undergone rapid transformation. There are several examples in agricultural settlements that illustrate these changes. For example, rural houses that were traditionally made of mud brick walls had open spaces for animals, including water buffaloes and cows. Adobe brick walls are now being replaced by firebrick walls that are able to support several floors. The growing population has reduced the amount of land available for agriculture, and firebrick homes have greatly helped farmers. In addition to this new construction, the recent introduction of mechanized farm equipment has transformed farmer's responsibilities. For example, machines have greatly diversified farming in rural Egypt and this has enabled farmers to have multiple roles outside their primary farming duties. They are now able to hold other jobs and still farm. Thus, there is a transformation of the farmer's role from a basic producer to an agricultural manager who is able to provide several services. The growth of urban development has encouraged rural people to seek higher paying jobs. They have been successful in obtaining jobs in the oil industry, in such urban areas as Cairo and Alexandria. When they return to their villages, their homes are remodeled based on urban designs. Unfortunately, many people see this change as being a threat to the local folk culture and its traditional architecture.

To fully understand agricultural settlements in Egypt, one must understand the role played by Sharia Islamic law. According to this tradition, *waqf* (religious endowments) are revenues obtained through lands. Typically, a waqf is a piece of arable land, farm, or even an oasis. The money obtained through a waqf supports mosques and other religious activities. This form of local land management based on Islamic laws is probably the oldest such system in the world. Waqf is also an important means of issuing charity to the poor. For example, if the waqf is used to purchase agrarian lands, then the land itself cannot be sold. Instead, the produce from the land is given as charity and even the ownership follows inheritance laws. A continuous charity system is made possible with the waqf, which was one of the important philosophies established by the Prophet Muhammad. Most of the agrarian settlements and farmlands created with waqf endowments have a mosque within the village as its principal administrator.

The Sinai

The people living on the Sinai Peninsula occupy a location that has long been important in Egyptian affairs. Politically, the peninsula was part of Israel from 1967 to 1979, when Israel agreed to pull out of the region as part of the Israel-Egypt Peace Treaty. Much of the Sinai is bordered by water. The Mediterranean Sea forms the region's northern border. In the northwest, the Suez Canal links the Red Sea and Mediterranean. At the head of the Red Sea, the "Y"-shaped troughs occupied by the Gulf of Suez in the west and Gulf of Aqaba complete the water boundaries. People living in the southern reaches of the Sinai, in particular, have benefited greatly from their crossroads location. Strategically situated between Israel, Saudi Arabia, and the Mediterranean coast, the cultural interaction over the years has been quite remarkable.

More than a dozen different Bedouin tribes live scattered throughout the Sinai Peninsula. The Aleiqat is the oldest of the tribes. They are primarily found along the western coast of the peninsula. The largest Bedouin tribe is the Tiyaha, which occupies the eastern part of the region. Southern Sinai in particular is the home of the Towara, or Arabs of the Tor. Over the years, the Towaras have successfully managed to preserve political leadership by forming alliances with different groups that have occupied the Sinai for centuries before it was incorporated into Egypt.

Today, the Sinai has several attractions that lure foreign tourists. For instance, the southeastern city of Dahab offers excellent scuba diving. Farther south is Sharm El Sheikh, which was once a sleepy fishing community, but today is one of the most popular tourist destinations in Egypt. To its south is the Ras Mohamed National Park, one of the only such parks found in this region. All of these tourist attractions were promoted by the Egyptian government after the last Israelis left the Sinai in 1982. The eastern and southeastern coasts of Sinai are therefore important revenue generators for Egypt and these regions have been declared protected areas. In particular, the Nabq protected area is one of the largest in the region.

The introduction of modern popular culture, such as Western-modeled tourism in traditional Bedouin society in the Sinai, has come at a price. In 2004, for instance, a powerful bomb blast ripped through the southeastern coastal tourist resort town of Taba. This was seen as a wake-up call to the growing cultural divisions in the Sinai. On one hand, there were wealthy resorts that had international facilities and world-class attractions. But next to these tourist destinations are poor Bedouin communities that lack even a reliable supply of water and electricity. The Bedouin lifestyle has been transformed over the years due to the various shifts in political power. For instance, when the Israeli occupation began in 1967, tourism was not a major industry in the Sinai. Traditional folk culture—including nomadic herding, subsistence agriculture, and fishing—was key to the Bedouins' survival. Few cash-paying jobs existed. Some Bedouins found temporary jobs as tour guides, but little other employment was available. Today, the Bedouins are still controlled by local sheikhs, who continue to exert control over the local culture.

In recent years, several agricultural programs have helped the local cultures in the Sinai, including many Bedouin groups. The development of orchards has been one such initiative that has helped Bedouins earn a living and survive in mainstream Egyptian society. The people and culture in the Sinai Peninsula are the keepers of the folk culture of nomadic Egyptian society. With increasing modernity in the region, it will be interesting to watch the Bedouin transformation as they increasingly embrace the growing popular-culture based Egyptian way of life.

CHAPTER

5

Government and Politics

S ince the 1952 revolution, when Egypt threw off the colonial yoke and became truly free, this Arab giant has walked a tightrope in the international arena. It has stepped carefully between the superpowers, between the Arab East and the West, between secular and religious affairs within the country, and between confrontation and accommodation with its twentieth-century foe, Israel. The political challenges have been huge and the choices difficult. Egypt's leaders have been invested with the authority to back up their decisions.

EGYPTIAN POLITICS SINCE 1956

When Gamal Abdel Nasser became president in 1956, he resolved to make Egypt an important and independent power both within the region and among developing nations around the world. He called for "nonalignment," meaning that Egypt should not be subservient to the needs of either of the world's superpowers—the United States or the Soviet Union. He was also a spokesman for Arab nationalism, a movement that would bring together Arab nations as a collective counterweight against great power and Israeli interests in the region. To this end, Egypt was briefly unified with Syria as a single country called the United Arab Republic. Nasser found nonalignment difficult. Egypt needed a lot of money to build the Aswan High Dam and effectively had to choose between seeking money from the West or from the Soviet Union. Nasser chose the West, asking the United States and Great Britain for the necessary funds. Those countries responded with loan conditions that Nasser thought would hurt his standing as an independent, nonaligned leader. So, for many months he did not accept or reject the Western loan offer. By the time he finally did agree to its terms, the Western lenders, especially the United States, were so angry with Nasser that they withdrew the offer.

Momentous events followed. Nasser nationalized the Suez Canal, meaning that he took control of it away from the British and French and placed it in Egyptian hands. The money Egypt earned by charging tolls on ships passing through the canal would be used to pay for the construction of the Aswan High Dam. Egypt also sought funding and technical assistance for the dam from the Soviet Union, and for the next 15 years, Soviet influence in Egypt was very strong. Great Britain and France decided to confront Egypt militarily and sent troops into the Suez Canal Zone. Israeli forces also participated in the 1956 war against Egypt, especially to destroy Soviet weapons in the Sinai Peninsula that could be used against Israel. Within days, the three invading powers held the Sinai Peninsula and the Suez Canal. However, there was strong international condemnation of these military actions, particularly by the United States, and Great Britain, France, and Israel soon withdrew. The Suez Canal was now firmly and finally Egyptian, a great victory for the nationalist Nasser.

During the term of President Gamal Abdel Nasser (1954–70), Egypt developed a close relationship with the Soviet Union, which provided one-third of the funding for the Aswan High Dam in Upper Egypt. Nasser is pictured here with Soviet premier Nikita Khrushchev at the opening of the dam in May 1964.

The next war did not go Nasser's way. In 1967, Egypt received faulty intelligence information from the Soviet Union, indicating that Israeli troops were poised for an invasion of Syria. Egypt warned Syria of the threat, and declared the Gulf of Aqaba off-limits to Israeli shipping. Nasser also called for United Nations peacekeeping troops to leave the Sinai, where they had been stationed since the 1956 war. Israeli leaders interpreted all of these actions as signs that their Arab neighbors were about to attack and decided to strike first.

Israeli warplanes took to the skies on June 5, 1967, quickly destroying the Egyptian and Syrian air forces on their respective runways. Having established what military commanders call air superiority, Israeli forces also advanced rapidly on the ground. Within six days, Israeli troops captured huge chunks of territory. They gained control of all the Sinai Peninsula, right up to the Suez Canal. They also took control of the Gaza Strip, a sliver of land that had been controlled by Egypt since 1948 and had a large Palestinian population, and the Golan Heights, a Syrian highland region that overlooked northeastern Israel. The West Bank, that part of Jordan that lay west of the Jordan River, where the population was mostly Palestinian Arab, also fell to Israeli forces. Israel's capture of the West Bank also included the prize catch of the Old City of Jerusalem, which contains Judaism's holiest site—the Western Wall—as well as places sacred to Muslims and Christians. Now humiliated and defeated, Nasser tried to step down as Egypt's leader, but the public rallied behind him and he remained in office until his death in 1970.

Nasser was succeeded by his vice president, Anwar Sadat, another officer from the 1952 coup. President Sadat was widely predicted to be an inconsequential Egyptian leader, but he defied expectations with some bold and risky political moves. First, he expelled the Soviets from Egypt, severing his country's relationship with its Communist benefactor, and began seeking stronger ties with the West, particularly the United States. Second, he decided to shake up the stalemated political landscape of the Middle East by joining Syria in a surprise attack against Israel in October 1973. Egyptian forces made remarkable progress against strong Israeli defenses east of the Suez Canal and pushed well into the Sinai Peninsula. These gains were soon

In the late 1970s, Egyptian president Anwar Sadat entered into peace talks with Israel that ultimately led to the Israel-Egypt Peace Treaty of 1979. Sadat (center) is pictured here shaking hands with Prime Minister Menachem Begin of Israel during Sadat's historic trip to Israel in November 1977.

reversed as Israeli troops encircled and cut off the Egyptian Army within the Sinai. A cease-fire was declared. Egypt did not regain the Sinai Peninsula, but gained a moral victory for challenging Israel. And Egypt did obtain something from the conflict—renewed control of the Suez Canal, which had been closed to shipping since the 1967 war. Egypt now had a sorely needed source of money.

Sadat's last bold, risky step was to enter into peace talks with Israel. He decided to overcome the long-standing regional policy that no Arab nation should accept Israel's right to exist. In 1977, he flew to Israel, and television viewers around the world witnessed his historic handshake with Israeli prime minister Menachem Begin and other leaders. Within two years, Sadat, Begin, and U.S. president Jimmy Carter concluded an extraordinary agreement called the Camp David Accords (because it was negotiated at the U.S. presidential retreat at Camp David, Maryland). It was the first "land for peace" deal between Israel and an Arab neighbor, meaning Israel gave back some of the Arab land it had occupied in 1967 in exchange for peaceful relations with the Arab country. In this case, Israel gave the Sinai Peninsula back to Egypt. There were handsome financial rewards for Sadat's peacemaking. Egypt now once again controlled its Sinai oilfields and the potential tourism development sites along the Sinai coasts. The United States began giving Egypt about $2 billion in aid every year. This U.S. contribution continues today and ranks second only to Israel's annual aid package of about $3 billion. Egypt had now become a firmly pro-Western, "moderate" Arab country.

Peacemaking also cost Sadat, and to some extent Egypt, dearly. Egypt had been the figurative center of the Arab world and the headquarters of its diplomatic bloc, the Arab League. As punishment for Egypt's treaty with Israel, the Arab League expelled Egypt and relocated its headquarters. Most Arab countries also broke diplomatic ties with Egypt. Within the country, there was little heartfelt warmth about the treaty with Israel, and a state of "cold peace" settled in between the countries. Some Egyptians, particularly those who advocated a radical form of Islam as an alternative to Egypt's secular politics, denounced Sadat as an un-Islamic traitor who had sold out to Israel and the West. One such faction, Islamic Jihad, succeeded in assassinating President Sadat during a military parade in Cairo on October 6, 1981. He was succeeded by his vice president, Hosni Mubarak, who continues today as one of the world's longest-serving elected presidents. During his initial years in office, perhaps his most significant contribution was gaining Egypt's reinstatement in the Arab League in 1989. In fact, the league's headquarters returned to Cairo.

In his first term, Mubarak was viewed as a liberator. He freed several political prisoners and offered an avenue for discussion among his political rivals. One such group is the New Wafd Party, which was established in 1983, reviving the old Wafd Party that was disbanded in the 1952 revolution. The New Wafd Party is seen as the liberal democratic Islamic party and a major rival to Mubarak's National Democratic Party (NDP). A constitutional restriction had allowed the Egyptian People's Assembly to elect a president. Thus, Mubarak has been reelected four times over the last two decades. In an effort to reduce international concerns over his authoritarian regime, in 2005, President Mubarak facilitated a constitutional amendment that allowed parties to run against the incumbent president. In the same year, the detention of Dr. Ayman Nour, a dissident candidate of the Al-Ghad Party, made countries including the United States question Mubarak and his government's commitment to free elections. News of illegal votes in rural Egypt prompted Nour to challenge the election results, which led to his imprisonment. Despite his extended rule over Egypt, President Mubarak has enjoyed the confidence of most Egyptians.

At the leadership level, an aging Mubarak is facing growing pressure from both within and outside of Egypt to select his successor. Many believe that his younger son, Gamal Mubarak, may succeed him. In almost every Egyptian government office and public service enterprise, a son usually takes over the position vacated by his father.

Egypt has experienced political changes due to two major political forces—the military and the Islamic groups, or Islamists. Another significant rival to President Mubarak's National Democratic Party is al-Ikhwan, or the Muslim Brotherhood. The 2005 parliamentary elections gave the Muslim Brotherhood a majority in Parliament. They have since forged a strong alliance with other Islamist organizations, including Hamas, thus increasing the influence of Islamic forces in shaping Egyptian politics.

Egypt, unlike Saudi Arabia, has a polarized Islamic society. The mainstream urban society has benefited from a liberalized economy and free entry of Western cultural traits. President Mubarak supports the growing population of young citizens and the need to give more rights to women. The more traditional Muslim Brotherhood occupies the other end of the spectrum—it continues to attempt to Islamize Egypt through the application of stricter Islamic Sharia codes of law. Only time will tell if the two forces will indeed come together, or whether political extremism will prevail.

POLITICAL STRUCTURE

Egypt is officially a democracy. But its citizens enjoy few of the democratic freedoms and little of the representation found in Western democracies, and Egypt's political system is usually described as authoritarian. There is a president who is nominated by the People's Assembly, or Parliament. Following the nomination, the president is elected for a six-year term in a popular referendum. In essence, the Egyptian people are asked to answer "yes" or "no" to the question: "Do you want this man to be your president?" Every six years, the answer is a resounding "yes," typically around 95 percent. There are many questions about how well the reported result reflects real feelings among Egyptians, and there are larger questions about Egypt's democratic process. Mubarak has been nominated repeatedly by his National Democratic Party, whose overwhelming grip on power within Parliament (holding about 95 percent of the seats) often seems to come about through suspect ways. Recent parliamentary elections have been accompanied by widespread voter fraud, including the stuffing of some ballot boxes and the suspicious disappearance of others, and the arrest and harassment of opposition supporters just prior to elections. Leading intellectuals have been jailed for encouraging Egyptians to vote for opposition candidates—and even for simply encouraging them to vote. Sometimes opposition candidates have boycotted the elections to express their unhappiness with what they believe to be a corrupt political system and election process.

As mentioned, there are legitimate opposition parties in Egypt, but they are not allowed to gain enough strength to threaten the seat of power. The New Wafd Party is the largest of these. Its members, including Coptic Christians, businessmen, former military officers, Islamists, and onetime supporters of President Nasser, are mainly from the middle and upper classes. Another opposition party is the Socialist Labor Party, which has many members who support the development of a more Islamic way of governing Egypt. There is also a mainly Marxist party called the National Progressive Unionist Grouping.

President Mubarak can appoint a vice president, but it is a telling indication of Egypt's authoritarian political system that he never has. Ever since he came to office with the assassination of President Sadat in 1981, Mubarak has ruled Egypt with emergency powers granted to him by Parliament. These powers suspend many of the freedoms that typically exist in a democracy and are justified on the grounds of maintaining security within the country. Real threats to that security, and certainly to the Mubarak regime, do exist, and most of them are in the form of Islamist opposition. For several decades now, that opposition has been Egypt's most serious political problem.

RELIGION AND POLITICS

A careful distinction must be made between *Islamic* and *Islamists*. Most Egyptians are Muslims who lead an Islamic way of life. They observe the five pillars of the faith, practice acts of kindness, and generally are tolerant of other faiths. But they also believe that the country and society should be organized along secular, rather than religious, lines. There are a small number of Muslims within Egypt who are Islamists. Their slogan is "Islam is the answer," meaning that all of the country's

The Muslim Brotherhood, which was founded in 1928, is the oldest and largest Islamist group in Egypt. Here, members of the Muslim Brotherhood hold up a banner emblazoned with their slogan, "Islam is the Solution," as they participate in a march in support of Makrem el-Deiri, the party's candidate during the 2005 elections.

and society's problems, particularly poverty and the lack of political participation, can be solved by adopting Islamic law as the law of the land and substituting religious for secular institutions at most levels. A wide range of Islamist opinions and organizations exist in Egypt, but their fundamental message is that the current government is politically illegitimate, too pro-Western, too accommodating to Israel, and not sufficiently Islamic, and therefore should be replaced.

The oldest and largest of the estimated 30 to 60 Islamist movements in Egypt is the aforementioned Muslim Brotherhood, founded in 1928. The organization made an attempt on the life of President Nasser, resulting in his cracking down on it. President Sadat allowed the Muslim Brotherhood more freedom, and the movement has continued to gain support during the Mubarak years. The breadth of this support is difficult to estimate, especially because the government has restricted the movement's freedom. It is a mainstream and moderate movement, especially when compared with some of Egypt's other Islamist groups. These include Islamic Jihad, which assassinated President Sadat in retaliation for his peacemaking with Israel, and the al-Gama'at al-Islamiyya (Islamic Group), which carried out a series of attacks on foreign tourists in Egypt in the 1990s. In striking at Egypt's vital tourist industry, these militants hoped to destabilize and perhaps cause the downfall of the Mubarak regime. Millions of Egyptians depend economically in some way on tourism. For this reason, the Islamic Group lost much popular sympathy when, in 1997, it carried out a gruesome assault on foreign tourists at an ancient Egyptian temple in Luxor resulting in the deaths of 58 people. Prior to that, Egypt's Islamists had enjoyed growing public support by coming to the aid of Egyptians in need. In the wake of the 1992 Cairo earthquake, for example, the group provided emergency services while the government response was slow and inadequate.

The Muslim Brotherhood, founded in Egypt by Hasan al-Banna, is the largest Sunni revival movement. Al-Banna was a visionary who was among the first major Islamic leaders to call for an all-inclusive Islamic society. His teachings in the 1930s and 1940s rekindled efforts to improve Egypt's public health, natural resources management, and social conditions. Both Arab and many non-Arab countries embraced the Muslim Brotherhood and al-Banna's leadership, because of its strong anticolonial beliefs. Al-Banna believed that in creating an Islamic state, there are a series of developmental measures that must be followed. He believed that the key to success begins with the Muslim individual, followed by the Muslim family, and finally Muslim society. Al-Banna believed that if these three stages were stable, then a society based on Islam and Sharia law could be achieved politically, thereby gaining cultural control of society. According to the Muslim Brotherhood, daily life must play a very important role in the development of an Islamic nation. In recent years, the Muslim Brotherhood has gained strength, especially after the 2005 elections in which it captured key seats in Parliament. Their victory was also coincidental with the Hamas victory in Palestine. Since then, a pan-Islamic relationship between the Muslim Brotherhood and Hamas has been growing. The Muslim Brotherhood has a strict hierarchy and a statelike structure, in which the "president" is the leader.

An important relationship exists between Egypt's political parties (and especially the Muslim Brotherhood) and the nation's most important religious institution, al-Azhar University. The university is one of the world's oldest, having been founded in A.D. 971 by the Fatimids. It is the most prestigious school in the Muslim world and can be compared to Oxford or Harvard in the Western world. Among the institution's key objectives is the promotion of Islamic teachings in the Arabic language. Islamic scholars, or *ulemas*, manage the curriculum and are responsible for the appropriate Islamic instructions. The role of the ulemas is prescribed in the *Qur'an* (the holy book of Islam) and calls for authorized Islamic leaders to deliver the words of the Prophet Muhammad and the Qur'an. Another core objective of the Muslim Brotherhood is the spread of *da'wa* as an important path toward Islamization and protection of the faith in the changing Egyptian society. This, too, is a responsibility vigorously promoted by al-Azhar University.

Looking ahead, the rising power of the Muslim Brotherhood will not support an attempt by President Mubarak to nominate his son Gamal as his successor. Politically, the role played by the Muslim Brotherhood will be critical not only to President Mubarak's National Democratic Party, but to Egypt's future as well. The Egyptian people are always watching the two parties quite closely. The Muslim Brotherhood has adapted itself to the changing trends of Egyptian society and has attempted to accommodate several views as envisioned by its founder, al-Banna. Moderate Egyptian Muslims believe that if the leaders at al-Azhar, a very influential Egyptian force, turn toward radical Islam, it will have a profound influence on the role of the Muslim Brotherhood and therefore Egypt's politics.

Finally, another important Islamist group influencing Egypt's politics is al-Gama'at al-Islamiyya. This group is not necessarily connected with the Muslim Brotherhood; rather, it is composed of a newer breed of Muslim leaders who represent a generation that has experienced more of the Mubarak regime than of Nasser. Unlike the Muslim Brotherhood, which seeks political legitimacy and tolerance with the entire Islamic world, al-Gama'at al-Islamiyya is more radical. In fact, on several occasions the Muslim Brotherhood has condemned its actions, especially the 1993 assassination attempt of an Egyptian government minister.

There are some strong links between these militant Islamist organizations in Egypt and the events leading up to and following the attacks on New York City and Washington, D.C., in September 2001. Ayman al-Zawahiri, the onetime physician who became the right-hand man of Osama bin Laden in the al-Qaeda organization, was jailed for his role in the Islamic Jihad's assassination of President Sadat. Islamic Jihad's spiritual leader, a blind cleric named Omar Abd al-Rahman, was convicted and imprisoned in the United States for his involvement in the first attack on New York's World Trade Center, in 1993. The actions of these men suggest that to some extent, Egypt was successful in exporting its Islamist problem abroad, by deporting the militant leaders or allowing them to relocate. As early as the 1980s, some went to Afghanistan to join the ranks of the "Afghan Arabs" who helped locals fight and eventually expel the Soviet invaders from Afghanistan. The Islamist victory against a powerful enemy gave much confidence to the

Human rights groups have often criticized the Egyptian government for repressing its citizens' civil liberties. Pictured here are members of the Movement for Change, or Kifaya, which supports democratic reforms and opposes the policies of President Hosni Mubarak.

fighters, and in time they sought more ambitious targets and recruited more followers, especially from Egypt. In the political vacuum that followed the Soviet withdrawal, Afghanistan became a kind of haven for Islamist militants training to overthrow their main enemies. Their hostility was directed toward the autocratic governments of the Middle East, including Egypt and Saudi Arabia; the country of Israel; and the United States, the nation that had, since 1990, stationed troops in Islam's holy land of Saudi Arabia.

Egypt has used means other than deportation to deal with its Islamist problem. Since coming to office, President Mubarak has carried out a virtual war against the more militant groups. Egypt has an extraordinary security apparatus, with informants and agents at every level of society. While the militants have carried out successful attacks, many of their efforts have undoubtedly been thwarted by the numerous arrests based on information provided by Egyptian security. Human rights groups complain about the state's heavy-handedness against Islamist suspects, and there are widespread reports of torture, along with the routine detention in jail without speedy trial. When legal action finally comes, it is often severe; scores of convicted Islamists have been executed. The country's reputation for human rights and civil liberties is generally poor. This is in part because of government restrictions on freedom of the press. But the government also makes it very difficult for nongovernmental organizations (NGOs)—including human rights and other "watchdog" groups—to form.

A CONTRACT WITH THE PEOPLE

Egypt has one of the world's oldest, largest, and perhaps most inefficient government bureaucracies. The government provides numerous services but often of poor quality. The country is only gradually changing from a mainly socialist state—in which the government owns and operates most businesses and services—to a mostly capitalist state in which private institutions perform all but the essential national functions. (The economic aspects of Egypt's transformation from socialism to capitalism are discussed in the next chapter.)

Egypt's government has an agreement with its people: It will take care of them. It tries to be a welfare state by promising every Egyptian that no matter what else is going on in the country or abroad, the government will try to help feed, clothe, and house its people. It also will provide for their medical needs, produce in factories what they need to consume, educate them (even college tuition is free at the public universities), guarantee them work in the government if they get college degrees, and help transport them to work. In this contract with the people, the government wants to ensure that Egyptians are not denied social services and that there will never be hunger, epidemic, or widespread illiteracy. To some extent the system is successful. Egypt does not have famines, for example, and indices of quality of life such as literacy and life expectancy are better now than they were before the 1952 revolution. The poorest people have been able to afford the basic necessities of life, especially staple food items. And students who complete their college degrees do get jobs.

The problem is that the contract between the government and the citizens is not fulfilled very effectively. Although the prices of some basic food items are kept artificially low so that poor people can afford them, they are still relatively expensive. Medical care is often inadequate—equipment is broken or outdated, and the best doctors may be found only in private practice, where their fees are too high for most people to afford. College graduates typically join the ranks of millions of other employees. They are jammed into already bloated government offices where there is little work to do and there are few rewards for work done—salaries are very low. Visitors to Egypt would almost certainly have at least one experience dealing with the government bureaucracy. A simple piece of paperwork—like extending a tourist visa to stay in the country—would lead the visitor through an incredibly complex and time-consuming series of visits to different offices within the giant *Mugamma* building in downtown Cairo. People would look the document over and put stamps on the application. It might seem that few of the people in these offices are doing any serious work, and most are sitting idly, drinking tea, or conversing. It is not a mistaken impression. The system is not supposed to work efficiently because if it did, there would not be work for many of these people. There is a saying that relates to the socialist system in the former Soviet Union that applies well to the Egyptian government employees: "The government pretends to pay us, and we pretend to work." This kind of experience in Egypt can be frustrating for both the person seeking help and the office workers. But do not forget that the United States also has a formidable bureaucracy—think about filing income tax, or what an Egyptian has to go through to get a visa to visit the United States.

Egypt provides one of the most liberal environments for women in the entire Arab world. Equal status to males and a variety of civil rights were made possible by the women's rights movement that began in the mid-1980s. In recent years, several women's groups have prompted the Egyptian government to recognize the role played by women and have encouraged their participation as well. A key factor in this revival has been broadcasting that emphasizes the importance of Sharia. Islamic law provides equal opportunity to men and women. It also applies to nearly all aspects of Egypt's Islamic society. In the last few years, the rights of women and their children have been protected by a series of constitutional amendments. For example, community services and legal assistance were made available to divorced women. And in 2003, President Mubarak appointed Tahany al-Gebaly as the first female chief justice of Egypt's Supreme Court, thereby opening a new door of opportunity for women.

CHAPTER

6

Egypt's Economy

Egypt is a developing country that desperately wants to become more industrialized and wealthy. But the country is finding it difficult to develop because of its growing population, a shortage of natural resources, and management problems. It is not among the world's poorest countries, like many of those to the south in Africa. Neither is it among the rather well-to-do developing countries such as Malaysia and South Korea. It is in the middle ranks of less-developed countries. A reliable measure of its wealth—in 2006, $4,200 per capita on the gross national income purchasing power parity scale—puts it on about the same scale of living as Cuba, Syria, Serbia, and Angola. Statistics tell a grim economic story. About 10 percent of the workforce is unemployed, although a much higher percentage is underemployed (employed less than full time or to their potential). Twenty-percent of the population lives below the poverty line. On the positive side, an estimated 40 percent of the population has reached the middle class, and 10 percent are wealthy.

SOURCES OF REVENUE

Egypt is not an important manufacturing country on the world stage. It is not a major exporter of brand-name consumer electronics and automobiles or industrial components such as iron and steel. Its main sources of revenue are from international tourism, oil exports, transit fees charged to ships that pass through the Suez Canal, and the money sent home by Egyptians working abroad. Each of these deserves a closer look.

Tourism is sometimes Egypt's most valuable source of foreign currency—the "hard" money it needs, because its own currency, the Egyptian pound (E£), is not convertible outside Egypt. Tourism is also a vulnerable industry for Egypt, thus the qualification that it is "sometimes" number one. The country has tremendous tourist attractions: the pyramids and other magnificent ancient monuments; the tranquility and romance of the Nile River; the impressive wilderness mountains of Sinai; the rich coral reefs lying off of sun-baked beaches; and the charm and hospitality of the Egyptians themselves. Tourists have been coming to Egypt for more than 3,000 years and going home to spread the word about the country's wonders.

When foreign travelers believe they are safe, Egypt's tourism has been successful. In 2000, tourism brought in $4.3 billion, accounting for about 11 percent of Egypt's gross domestic product. More than 2 million Egyptians have jobs directly related to tourism, and millions more receive some trickle-down benefit from the money foreign tourists spend. But those livelihoods and benefits are unreliable. Whenever there is a terrorist incident in Egypt, in the Middle East, or abroad (but with connections to the Middle East), tourism to Egypt drops off. It usually rebounds, but only slowly. The most serious downturn in tourism came after the attacks on the United States in

Tourism is one of Egypt's primary sources of revenue. Unfortunately, whenever there is a terrorist incident in the country or in the Middle East, the industry is adversely affected. Here, a group of tourists pose for a photo in front of the Giza Pyramids, near Cairo.

September 2001. By October of that year, tourism had dropped by nearly 50 percent. That was on top of already steep declines following an escalation of tensions between Israel and Palestinians beginning in August 2000. Following the 2001 attacks, hotels, airlines, and cruise ships cut prices dramatically and sought more budget-minded tourists, especially from Russia.

Oil is a more reliable, although finite, resource, and Egypt has only modest petroleum reserves. And oil, too, is subject to the whims of global events. Most of the country's oil is around and below the Gulf of Suez, especially along the west coast of the Sinai Peninsula (that is one reason President Sadat wanted to win back the peninsula from Israel). Egypt is not a member of the Organization of Petroleum Exporting Countries (OPEC), the 12-nation member cartel that has the biggest role in deciding global production and pricing of oil. But like the OPEC members, Egypt benefits when the price of oil is reasonably high and suffers when the price declines. Egypt had an especially bad budget situation in the late 1980s, when the price of oil sank to as low as $9 per barrel. It was doing well in 2000, when the price was around $30 per barrel. But then the terrorist attacks on the United States sent many economies around the world into recession. Industrial production slowed down, meaning less oil was needed. So the price of oil fell, and Egypt saw less revenue. By 2006, with oil prices exceeding $60 a barrel, Egypt's economy was once again benefiting greatly from its petroleum resources.

Not as profitable as oil, but a steadier source of income, is the fee Egypt charges to each ship passing through the Suez Canal. Oil tankers once made up the most important traffic through the canal. When fighting between Egypt and Israel closed the canal in 1973, however, a new generation of supertankers was built to carry Middle Eastern oil by sea around Africa to western Europe and North America. When the canal reopened in 1975, it was not wide and deep enough to accommodate these huge vessels. Egypt is now enlarging the canal to take in those ships. In 2006, the country earned approximately $3.6 billion in fees.

Remittances are the last of Egypt's four main revenue earners. This involves money earned by Egyptians working abroad and then carried or sent home to where it is spent. Strangely, this income source is a mixed blessing. On the one hand, it is the result of a "brain drain." Some of the best and brightest Egyptian engineers and doctors, for example, are working abroad and therefore not helping their country to develop at home. On the other hand, Egypt simply does not have enough available jobs, or sufficiently attractive salaries for these professionals to keep them home. The oil-wealthy countries of the

Persian Gulf, such as Saudi Arabia, Kuwait, and the United Arab Emirates, employ most of the skilled and unskilled Egyptian workers. Their salaries are usually much higher than they would be in Egypt, and when they come home they have not only money in their pockets, but typically consumer electronics and other luxuries purchased in the Persian Gulf States.

There is also considerable foreign aid pouring into Egypt, with the main donors and lenders being the United States and the European Union. The United States provides about $2 billion worth of aid to Egypt each year. Some of this goes toward improving the country's poor infrastructure, including its drinking water and sewage systems. Much, however, is military aid—new fighter jets and other war material, for example— that is of little apparent benefit to the Egyptian people. Critics of foreign aid point out that it comes with many strings attached. For example, the engineering firms hired to build the new sewage facilities are American, so much of the money goes back to the United States. There are also international agencies like the International Monetary Fund (IMF) and World Bank that lend money for Egypt to invest in development projects. It is sometimes difficult for Egypt to keep up with the payments on these loans, and pressure from the lenders forces Egyptian leaders to make difficult and unpopular decisions.

DOMESTIC POLICY

The most famous example of a tough and unpopular decision was President Sadat's 1977 decree that the subsidies on bread and other basic food items should be cut. Subsidies are the monies the government pays to make items available to the public at below-market cost. Such assistance has long been part of the covenant between Egypt and its people. In 1977, the IMF pressured the Egyptian government over its loan, which led Sadat to cut the expensive subsidies. The prices of bread, rice, cooking oil, and other staples shot up immediately by almost 40 percent. Egyptians immediately took to the streets in harsh protest. They burned nightclubs, railway cars, and government buildings; they also overturned cars, attacked foreign airline offices, and generally wreaked havoc until, within hours, the government backed down and restored the subsidies. There were some fatalities and many injuries. After the January 1977 food riots, the government has proceeded cautiously in carrying out economic reforms that would potentially hurt the poor.

Around the time of the food riots, President Sadat instituted a new economic policy for Egypt that was meant to improve the country's standard of living and give it some footing on the international economic stage. It was called the *infitah*, meaning "opening"—Egypt's doors would now be opened to foreign investment. Up to that time, almost all of Egypt's industries were state-run. They produced few export goods and few consumer products that Egyptians wanted to buy. The open door was supposed to change that, inviting international businesses to take advantage of Egypt's abundant and well-trained workforce to manufacture products for foreign and local consumption. So far, infitah has resulted in only modest progress. There are consumer goods—almost any convenience of modern life can be purchased in Egypt today—but most are imported. The hoped-for emergence of a dynamic, private manufacturing sector has not taken place. Many foreign businesses are put off by the risks of investing in the volatile Middle East, by the red tape involved in setting up shop in Egypt, and by the kickbacks that, although not legal, have to be paid for things to work properly.

In the Egyptian economy, influence (called *wasta*) is what often gets things done. Wasta can simply mean having the right connections, like having personal or business ties that make it easy to win a contract, for example. It can mean paying the kickbacks or bribes that can grease the wheels if a businessman lacks personal connections. And wasta is part of Egypt's *bakshiish* economy. Bakshiish means "tip," but it is often expected even if no service is provided, or to supplement the income of a person providing a service. For example, a visitor would pay admission to visit an ancient Egyptian monument and then would pay bakshiish—perhaps a dollar—to the site's guard, who would show some of its attractions (whether the visitor wanted him to or not). Few foreigners traveling in Egypt ever get mad about paying out such trifling amounts to Egyptians, particularly when they appreciate how meager their incomes are.

Most Americans would have a hard time imagining how Egyptians get by on their salaries. Typical middle-class salaries range between $100 and $400 per month (of course the costs of living are much lower than in the United States). Many people work second jobs, such as driving taxis. There also are some very rich people in Egypt. One of the criticisms of Sadat's infitah policy, and of Egypt today, is that a select few have enriched themselves with lucrative business contracts, while the masses have lost ground, or have failed to make progress economically. The apparent disparities between the haves and have-nots in Egypt have grown. The visitor to Egypt sees flashy Mercedes cars and other showy signs of wealth, appearing quite out of place where city and village people struggle to make a living. While living space is notoriously cramped, costly, and difficult to find for the great majority of Egyptians, a select few have second and even third summer or winter homes in the countryside. There are fears that at some point popular resentment against the wealthy class could turn into a raging civil conflict.

AGRICULTURE

Egypt is of course an agricultural country—most of its people are rural—and one would expect farming to be among its leading economic assets. Egypt's fertile soils near the Nile River produce cereals (mainly wheat, maize, rice, and barley), cotton, and sugarcane. Many vegetables also are grown (notably tomatoes, eggplant, cucumber, spinach, beans, okra, and onions), as are fruits (especially oranges, tangerines, lemons, apricots, grapes, bananas, and mangoes), and forage plants. Cotton, rice, and maize (corn) are the leading commercial export, or cash,

Cotton is one of Egypt's primary exports: Profits often top a billion dollars and the industry employs more than one million Egyptians. Here, tenant-farmers harvest cotton in the delta region north of Cairo.

crops. Egypt was once a considerable exporter of these and other agricultural products. Since the 1970s, however, Egypt has imported more food than it has exported, and the imbalance in favor of imports is growing steadily (food makes up more than 30 percent of Egypt's import expenditures). Most of the wheat, the country's staple cereal, for example, comes from the United States. The basic problem is the one that bedevils almost every effort Egypt makes to develop: For decades, population growth has outstripped economic development.

Egypt's approach to the population/economic growth dilemma has long been to try to increase the number of crops grown on its agricultural land and to expand its land area in cultivation. The biggest effort was the construction of the Aswan High Dam, which has been a mixed blessing for Egypt. On the plus side, it converted about a million acres (405,000 hectares) of land in the Nile Valley and the Nile Delta from seasonal to perennial irrigation, meaning that two or three crops, instead of just one, could be grown each year. The area under cultivation has also increased by about a million acres, especially through the reclamation of desert land: With more water available, it became possible to irrigate the desert fringes of the Nile Valley and delta, particularly the area just west of the delta, between Cairo and Alexandria. Hydroelectricity for the country's commercial and residential needs is produced at the dam's power station (it generates about 25 percent of the country's electricity). The dam also prevents destructive floods and provides water during periods of drought.

On the negative side, farmers tend to overuse the always-available water, therefore accidentally adding too much salt to their fertile land (the salts are contained in the water and are left behind as the water evaporates). Farmers now have to buy expensive artificial fertilizers because the free fertilizer provided by the Ethiopian silt is now locked up behind the dam. Those silts gave nourishment to sardines in the Mediterranean Sea, off the shore of the Nile Delta, but the sardine fishing industry has come to an end because the silts are gone. Mediterranean Sea water has begun to erode land from the Nile Delta, because the silts are not rebuilding the delta's headland. Land reclamation has proven disappointing. Just getting water to the desert does not make its sands fertile. The inputs have been costly and the returns few. Comprising about 13 percent of Egypt's total cultivated area, reclaimed lands contribute only 2 percent of the nation's total agricultural output. Many of Nubia's archaeological monuments were covered by Lake Nasser, or, like Abu Simbel, had to be relocated to higher ground. Overall, however, Egyptians defend the decision to build the Aswan High Dam and argue that its benefits outweigh its problems.

CONSERVATION AND RECLAMATION

Water management and conservation are key in a nation where the majority of the land area is arid. In Egypt, water resources and irrigation are concentrated along the Nile River region. In recent times, however, rural communities in southern and western regions of the nation have been in greater need of irrigation water. Growing water demands and the future of Egypt's water management perhaps can best be resolved by falling back upon traditional Islamic principles. As one would expect from a faith founded in an arid land, Sharia, the Islamic law, extends into water-use policies. For example, it emphasizes the importance of water conservation, stressing that its use must benefit the larger community. In recent times, the Gulf Cooperation Council, which works closely with Egypt, has also promoted public awareness in water management by incorporating Islamic teachings.

Land reclamation west of the Nile Delta has been one of the multipronged efforts Egypt has undertaken to conquer and develop its deserts. Another is to increase cultivation and settlement in what Egyptians call the New Valley (*Wadi Gadeed*), the oases depressions of Kharga and Dakhla. They are judged to be underpopulated relative to the Nile Valley and delta, and so efforts are under way to draw settlers from the overcrowded Nile region by developing petroleum and mineral industries and increasing the cultivable area of these oases—mainly by drilling new wells, but also recently by bringing freshwater from Lake Nasser by canal in the so-called Tushka Project. Another canal carries Nile water from the eastern delta into the northern Sinai Peninsula, where there are plans to resettle as many as a million inhabitants from the Nile region.

Still another effort focuses on the satellite cities, a series of new settlements constructed in desert areas, especially east and west of the Nile Delta. These were meant to relieve one of Egypt's great problems, the urban primacy of Cairo. The country's capital is a classic primate city, meaning Cairo has more people than Egypt's second- and third-largest cities combined. Practically everything and everybody gravitates to Cairo, because that is where most of the country's jobs and services are located. The problem is that such urban primacy has a snowball effect: The opportunities attract more and more people, and the city keeps growing, so the government pours

Cairo is the home of Africa's only subway system, which was built in the late 1980s. Known as "The Metro," the subway system carries between 2.5 and 3 million people each day. Here, workers help build the city's first subway tunnel under the Nile River in 1998.

more and more resources into trying to keep up with the growing population. Cairo's impressive new subway system is part of that effort.

FURTHER DEVELOPMENT

All of that attention to Cairo means that development elsewhere in the country is being neglected, and the increasing crowding and pollution in Cairo reduces the quality of life there. Meanwhile, Cairo's expansion is actually eating up quality farmland in a country that cannot afford to lose any. The satellite cities were meant to tackle these problems: New jobs and services would be created in them so that people would not have to move to Cairo. They would relieve the crowding in the Nile Valley and not consume farmland, and they would offer people cleaner air and greater quality of life than Cairo does. The problem has been that not enough people want to live in these new desert cities. Despite the lower costs of living and their other amenities in the desert, Egyptians prefer to live in the Nile area—and especially in Cairo—where the action is. Egyptian distaste for the desert goes back to Pharaonic times, and it is a deep-seated cultural preference that has been hard to change.

Egypt also has a significant fishing industry that is important for three key reasons. First, many of the coastal communities bordering the Red Sea and Mediterranean coast depend on income from fishing. It also is important to millions of residents living along the Nile River. Second, fishing represents a traditional folk economic activity that has been practiced for millennia. Finally, fish provide a "free" source of protein to many people who, because of their poverty, otherwise would be hard-pressed to obtain meat. During recent decades, some environmental problems have emerged that affect fishing. For instance, the Aswan Dam has blocked nutrients that previously were discharged into the Nile Delta and Mediterranean. This has caused several species of economically viable fish to disappear. Inland lakes including Lake Nasser and Lake Qarun have been sources of fish for the interior regions, although increased salinization has caused a sharp decline in the fish yield of Lake Qarun. Fish is an important item in the diet of many Egyptians and modern technologies including deep freezing and salting techniques have helped fish consumption to spread even to the rural interior.

In recent years, Egypt has been trying to negotiate a free trade agreement with the United States. Egypt is in a splendid position to accept economic reforms, and free trade is bound to improve its economy, according to some estimates by more than 3 percent per year. However, political obstacles have hindered Egyptian involvement. Inconsistencies in the Egyptian democratic structure and President Mubarak's extended reign as the country's leader, for example, have delayed negotiations. In 2005, Mubarak's decision to allow multiparty elections improved his country's chances, but the arrest of his lone opponent, Ayman Nour, created a huge stumbling block to Egypt's entry into a free trade agreement.

Egypt faces many problems, but one could convincingly argue that none is greater than the need for economic development. As an economy develops, of course, not all people prosper. It can take centuries for a strong and viable middle class to develop. As is true in many developing countries, the divide between Egypt's rich and poor is quite evident. Dress, housing styles, means of transportation, and level of educational attainment are some of the "obvious" differences between rich and poor. The differences are particularly noticeable in Upper Egypt. Here, more than 65 percent of the people live below the poverty line. Landless farmers, unemployed youth and women, and predominantly small-scale farmers all contribute to the region's dismal economic conditions. Although most of the people here are traditional farmers, practicing archaic methods, the land is not well suited to crop production. Additionally, the scarcity of water resources and very small land holdings combine to make it extremely difficult for farmers to eke out enough production to feed their families and make an adequate income. The situation is much better in Lower Egypt, where ample water is available to irrigate the fertile soils of the Nile Delta.

7

Living in Egypt Today

Life in Egypt today is a series of challenges that most Egyptians take on with characteristic good humor. That sense of humor combined with extraordinary patience help Egyptians cope with conditions that could make many people break down in tears or cry out in anger. Overcrowding, the struggle to make a living, the burden of waiting for almost everything because too many people are trying to use limited services at the same time—these are features of everyday life that Egyptians shrug off as a part of life. Their faith and their strong sense of family and friendship give them that fortitude.

FAMILY

To grow up in Egypt is to grow up blessed with family. Kinship ties are extremely important. In American society, it is common for brothers and sisters to live in different cities if not different states, and for adult children to leave home, seeing their parents less frequently.

In Egypt, all family members try to stay in the closest contact possible, and it is considered an emotional hardship when sons or daughters go to live and work in distant cities or countries. Parents lavish enormous affection on their children—what Americans call "quality time" is the norm in the Egyptian family. Then children look after their parents when their turn comes. There are no retirement homes, and elderly parents are taken in and cared for by the children. Aunts, uncles, nephews, nieces, and cousins are also part of the daily scene in the Egyptian household.

Marriages are generally strong in Egypt; reflecting the value placed on family life. Divorce rates are very low relative to those in the United States. Gender roles are what Americans would call traditional. The man is expected to have the job, and the woman is expected to be the caretaker of the home and children. A lot of Egyptian women do work, particularly in the cities, but for many, the job ends with marriage.

Finding a spouse in Egypt is a different process than it is in the United States. Parents have much say in what partner a son or daughter should have. Sometimes they negotiate an arranged marriage, finding a suitable bride or groom based on kinship. Traditionally, the ideal marriage has been between first cousins: A man should marry his father's brother's daughter, or his mother's brother's daughter. These unions are infrequent enough that genetic consequences are limited. The closeness of this ideal arrangement is, however, a good indicator of how close kinship bonds are in Egypt.

In the arranged marriage, which is more common in villages than in cities, love is expected to develop over time. As Egyptians see it, this is far better than falling madly in love at first sight, only to discover incompatibilities over time, and a relationship ending in divorce. Where marriages are not arranged, there is dating, but it is quite different from typical courtship in the United States. For example, a son or daughter must get his or her parents' consent before going on a date.

In rural parts of Egypt, arranged marriages are quite common, particularly between first cousins. Here, a marriage procession moves along the banks of the Nile River near the town of Dendera.

The dates are chaperoned—a brother, uncle, or father accompanies the boy and girl to a movie or restaurant, for example. Premarital sex is frowned upon, particularly because it can bring dishonor to a family. Honor is extremely important in Egypt, as in all Arab societies, and illicit relationships are among the most dishonorable acts. (This helps explain Egypt's extremely low rate of HIV/AIDS, which affects less than 0.1 percent of the population.)

Boy meets girl and parents approve is not the end of the courtship story. From the start, the groom is expected to be able to accommodate and care for his bride financially. This can be a huge challenge in Egypt's difficult economy. The man has to find a secure job and then save enough money to be able to make a down payment on an apartment. This can take years, resulting in men marrying much later than they would without these requirements. It is also customary, especially in the villages, for the groom to present his wife with a dowry, often called a bride-price. This could be cash, livestock, or other assets and represents some initial wealth that the wife may exclusively claim as her own.

Friendship, like family, is a strong institution in Egypt. Men and women develop intensely close bonds with others that can last a lifetime. Friends often call each other brothers or sisters. It is very rare for a man to have a close woman friend, or vice versa. Gender distance and separation are encouraged or enforced at every stage of life in Egypt—boys and girls are often educated separately, and public facilities are often segregated by sex. This separation is in keeping with the general Islamic sense of honor and propriety. In recent years, there has been a growing embrace of fundamental Islamic values. For example, many more women wear the *hijab* (headscarf) now than a decade or two ago.

Just being with family and friends is the favorite activity of most Egyptians. They are an extremely sociable and outgoing people and regard Americans as rather shy and retiring in comparison. Egyptians do not hesitate to open up a friendly conversation with anyone, and their "personal space" is closer than it is among Americans. Men greet men with hugs and kisses. Their handshakes linger, or they hold hands. Women do the same, and there is no awkwardness about that—these are expressions of friendship in Egypt.

POPULAR CULTURE

Egypt is the music and film capital of the Arab world, and Egyptians are passionate about songs and movies. When the country's most beloved singer, Um Kalthum, died in 1975, there was an unprecedented national outpouring of grief. Her tapes are still best sellers in Egypt. Egyptian film stars—including Omar Sharif, who also made it big in Western film roles—are the country's biggest celebrities. There are theaters throughout the big cities, and video rentals are also strong. Most urban

The Feast of the Sacrifice, or Eid al-Adha, is the most important holiday in the Islamic calendar. The three-day feast is held during the month of Dhu'l-Hijja and commemorates Abraham's willingness to sacrifice his son Ishmael.

Egyptian homes have televisions and they are becoming more common in villages. Egyptians delight in soap operas, and recounting the actors' latest tribulations is a favorite topic of conversation. Educated Egyptians are avid readers, and Egypt boasts some of the Arab world's greatest writers. These include Naguib Mahfouz, a Nobel prizewinner whose translated works can be found in most bookstores in the United States.

Egyptians love sports, particularly soccer (which they, as do people throughout most of the world, call "football"). The rivalries between city soccer teams ignite passions among the fans, and the entire country rallies behind its national team during the World Cup, which takes place every four years. Egyptians are not great outdoors people. Hiking and camping, for example, are not popular activities, but they do enjoy day trips to Mediterranean or Red Sea beaches. There are also a few popular green spaces in Cairo, particularly the zoo.

As Egypt is predominately Muslim, the major holidays are Islamic: the *Eid al-Adha,* or Feast of the Sacrifice, following the conclusion of the annual pilgrimage to Mecca; and the *Eid al-Fitr,* or Feast of the Breaking of the Fast, following the end of the fast during the month of Ramadan. The Prophet Muhammad's birthday (*Mawlid an-Nabi*) is another important Muslim feast day. There are also pre-Islamic holidays, including the springtime festival called Sniffing the Breeze (*Sham el-Naseem*). During each of these holidays, large embroidered tents are erected on city streets, within which sweets, toys, and holiday decorations are sold.

FOOD

Almost every Egyptian has a sweet tooth. Even a cup of tea is prepared with a few heaps of sugar. The country's most widely consumed foods are boiled fava beans (*fuul*) and deep-fried chick peas (*taamiya*). Western fast-food restaurants, including McDonald's and KFC, are common in the bigger cities, but the traditional Egyptian fast foods are fuul, taamiya, and *kushri,* a spicy macaroni and lentil dish. Meats are too expensive for most people to consume frequently, but popular meat dishes are made from lamb or mutton and include *shawarma*—grilled lamb served with tomatoes on a hot bun.

Islamic traditions frown upon intoxicants, and alcoholism and drug use are rare in Egypt. Beer, wine, and spirits are offered only in tourist restaurants, and they are sold in a few government stores, or discreetly in some urban supermarkets.

HEALTH

Egyptians do have some health problems, however. Smoking is widespread among men. There are very few public restrictions or warnings about smoking, and although statistics are not available, cancer death rates are believed to be high. Egyptians enjoy a medium quality of life when compared with the other countries of the world. The average life expectancy is 72, compared with 78 in the United States, and 44 in Afghanistan. The United Nations' Human Development Index (2005) rates Egypt's overall quality of life as 119th out of the world's 177 countries (with Norway and Iceland as number one and number two, and Sierra Leone number 176 and Niger number 177). This index goes beyond simple per-capita gross national product or income standards to evaluate aspects of the human experience. It includes some two-dozen categories of well-being. Neither at the top nor at the bottom when measured by these standards, Egyptians know they could be better off, but they continue to make do—often very creatively and with a great sense of humor—with what they have. Visitors see immediately that Egyptians laugh a lot and enjoy exchanging jokes, even in the most trying circumstances—stuck in a traffic jam in Cairo, for instance, which is likely to be a visitor's first experience in the country!

That long ride from the Cairo airport to a hotel offers a microcosm of life in Egypt today. Typically, the driver is a middle-aged man with a university degree in engineering. He works at the Ministry of Agriculture in a desk job that pays him $75 a month, not nearly enough to keep up with rent, food, and clothing for his wife and five children. With the driving, he can earn a total of $200 a month. But he is not complaining so much as he is asking his passenger about where he is from and about his family. At the start of the ride, the driver may have said that the fare would be E£5, but by the end of the ride, the visitor may have to politely decline the driver's invitation to dine with him and his family, and the driver has refused to accept any payment. The visitor already feels very much at home.

CHAPTER

8

Egypt Looks Ahead

Moving forward, the people of this "antique land" are confronted with many local, regional, and global challenges to their well-being. The citizens and their political leaders are confronted by numerous and pressing social, economic, and political issues. This chapter provides a brief discussion of some of the steps that the majority of Egypt's observers insist the country should take if it is to move forward.

Egypt's most difficult problems are economic. Prospects for the country's poor, who make up half the population, have not improved in recent years. The middle class, too, has made little progress. Most of the economic benefits have gone to the wealthiest 10 percent of the population. Unless this widening gap begins to narrow, chances for political unrest and violence will increase. Observers agree that Egypt's government must do more to improve the lives of Egypt's underprivileged. More government jobs and services need to be created in the poorest parts of the country, particularly in the villages and towns of Upper (southern) Egypt. The government will have to preserve and even expand its social security net for the poor by subsidizing their basic food and clothing needs, rather than continue to look for ways to cut the subsidies. Presumably, reducing expenditures on defense could free up more money for this purpose. And, because much of Egypt's rural poverty is a result of too few agricultural resources, improvements in farming must be made. The continued expansion of cities and towns into Egypt's limited farmland must be stopped. The current emphasis on large-scale efforts to reclaim desert land should be reevaluated, because of the enormous cost and typically low returns of these projects. Worldwide experience suggests that more benefits may come from small-scale, local efforts to improve existing farming technology.

Perhaps the most serious threat to Egypt's economic well-being is population growth. Even though it has slowed markedly in recent decades, the population growth rate is still high, and Egypt's population is expected to grow by two-thirds in the next half century. This expected surge in people means that the country faces a huge struggle just to break even, much less gain ground economically. Again, more attention to the root problem of poverty is essential to reduce birthrates. Women, in particular rural women, need more education—there is a worldwide correlation between greater female literacy and lower birthrates. This will require some fundamental cultural changes. Parents will need to be convinced that their daughters can and should go to school—now they tend to hold the girls back with the belief that "their place is in the home" and therefore they need not be formally educated.

Egypt's past and potential domestic unrest also has roots in the country's poverty. Islamist extremism originated in Upper Egypt, the poorest part of the country, and made progress as extremists argued that Islamic law was the one true alternative to a political system that benefited mainly

Although Egypt's rate of population growth has dropped in recent years (it stood at 1.72 percent in 2007), it is still overcrowded, because many parts of the country are uninhabitable. There is a direct correlation between education and lower birthrates, and as more and more girls continue to attend school, Egypt's growth rate should continue to decline.

the wealthy. To defuse future Islamist revolts, the Egyptian government will have to do more than arrest and imprison Islamists, which is the main method used now. More genuine attention to the plight of the poor, and more concessions to the demands of moderate Islamists to participate in Egypt's political life, will be needed. Throughout the political spectrum there are pleas for greater freedom of expression and opportunities for political power. Egypt risks losing its place as the capital of Arab culture unless its intellectuals and artists are permitted to express themselves without fear of imprisonment. Political repression can also pose threats to government stability, as Islamists or others turn to violence as their only means of expression.

Egypt's central place in the regional and international strategic arena seems secure for the near future, but there are long-term dangers. The United States does not want this demographic giant of an estimated 80 million to become unfriendly to its interests and is likely to continue sending large amounts of economic aid to Egypt. The United States relies on Egypt in particular to mediate in the Israeli-Palestinian dispute, and as long as the conflict goes unresolved, the U.S.–Egypt economic partnership should be strong (ironically, then, regional peace could be bad economically for Egypt). At the same time, Egypt does not want to be seen by its Arab neighbors as a puppet of the United States. Its struggle to maintain some political independence from the United States may be seen in particular in Egypt's view of Iraq. Egypt was also slow to embrace any U.S. expansion outside Afghanistan of the war on terrorism following the September 11, 2001, attacks in which, as the opening of this book pointed out, some Egyptians were involved.

Egypt's future is dependent on several forces that have shaped the nation today. The September 11 attacks on the United States and the involvement of Egyptian nationals in the attacks attracted the world's attention. However, the Egyptian government has in fact been cracking down on Islamists for several years. The Muslim Brotherhood and the Egyptian government have rallied against terrorism. The post-9/11 timeline has also made Egypt's role in international politics even more important. With the Arab League based in Cairo and its ideal location situated at a crossroads between Europe, Africa, and the Middle East, Egypt has a major role in bridging the wide gap that exists between the Western and Arab worlds.

In particular, the country's political future may depend upon what happens after President Mubarak's long tenure as the nation's head of state comes to an end. The recent meeting by U.S. president George W. Bush with President Mubarak's son Gamal is seen as a sign that the United States approves of Gamal

Although the United States seems to support Hosni Mubarak's son Gamal as the likely successor to serve as Egypt's president, many political groups, including the Muslim Brotherhood, oppose the move. Here, Gamal Mubarak is pictured with Oscar-winning actor George Clooney in December 2006, during Clooney's visit to Egypt to gain support for the victims of the Darfur conflict in western Sudan.

taking over as successor. Gamal Mubarak is seen by many as an ideal successor, and he would be the first civilian head of state if indeed he becomes president. But it is unclear if he would be interested in the job; on more than one occasion, he has indicated that he has no desire to assume the country's highest office. The future of the Egyptian government could fall on the shoulders of the Muslim Brotherhood, if it is able to replace the National Democratic Party headed by President Mubarak.

During the 2005 parliamentary elections, the Muslim Brotherhood captured several seats in Parliament, which assured that Mubarak would face opposition for the first time since he became president in 1981. Although Mubarak was reelected in 2005, less than 25 percent of registered Egyptian voters turned out for the election. Surely more will participate in the next presidential election in 2011, when Mubarak seems likely to support his son Gamal for president.

Facts at a Glance

Physical Geography

Location Northeastern Africa, bordering the Mediterranean Sea, between Libya and the Gaza Strip, and the Red Sea north of Sudan, and includes the Asian Sinai Peninsula and southwest Asia (Sinai Peninsula)

Area Total: 386,662 square miles (1,001,450 square kilometers); *land:* 384,345 square miles (995,450 square kilometers); *water:* 2,317 square miles (6,000 square kilometers)

Boundaries *Border countries:* Gaza Strip, 6.8 miles (11 kilometers); Israel, 165 miles (266 kilometers); Libya, 693 miles (1,115 kilometers); Sudan, 791 miles (1,273 kilometers); *total:* 1,656 miles (2,665 kilometers)

Coastlines 1,613 miles (2,689 kilometers), on Mediterranean Sea, Gulf of Suez, Gulf of Aqaba, and Red Sea

Climate Desert; hot, dry summers with mild winters, rainy in north

Terrain Mountainous igneous rocks in Sinai and Eastern Desert; sedimentary plateaus in Western Desert; Nile Valley runs north-south through limestone plateau

Elevation Extremes Lowest point is Qattara Depression, 436 feet (133 meters) below sea level; highest point, Jebel Katarina, 8,625 feet (2,629 meters)

Land Use Arable land, 2.92%; permanent crops, 0.5%; other, 96.58% (2005)

Irrigated Land 13,212 square miles (34,220 square kilometers) (2003)

Natural Hazards Periodic droughts; frequent earthquakes, flash floods, landslides; hot, driving windstorm called khamsin occurs in spring; dust storms, sandstorms

Natural Resources Petroleum, natural gas, iron ore, phosphates, manganese, limestone, gypsum, talc, asbestos, lead, zinc

Environmental Issues Agricultural land being lost to urbanization and wind-blown sands; increasing soil salination below Aswan High Dam; desertification; oil pollution threatening coral reefs, beaches, and marine habitats; other water pollution from agricultural pesticides, raw sewage, and industrial effluents; very limited natural freshwater resources away from the Nile, which is the only perennial water source; rapid growth in population overstraining the Nile and natural resources

People

Population	80,335,036 (July 2007 est.); males, 40,499,507 (2007 est.); females, 39,835,529 (2007 est.)
Population Density	192 people per square mile (74 people per square kilometer)
Population Growth Rate	1.72% (2007 est.)
Net Migration Rate	-0.21 migrant(s)/1,000 population (2007 est.)
Fertility Rate	2.77 children born/woman (2007 est.)
Birthrate	22.53 births per 1,000 population (2007)
Death Rate	5.11 deaths per 1,000 population (2007)
Life Expectancy at Birth	Total population: 71.6 years; male, 69.0 years; female, 74.2 years (2007 est.)
Median Age	Total: 24.2; male, 23.9; female, 24.6 (2007 est.)
Ethnic Groups	Egyptian, 98%; Berber, Nubian, Bedouin, and Beja, 1%; Greek, Armenian, other European (primarily Italian and French), 1%
Religion	Muslim (mostly Sunni), 90%; Coptic Christian, 9%; other Christian, 1%
Language	Arabic (official), English and French widely understood by educated classes
Literacy	(Age 15 and over can read and write) Total population: 71.4% (83%, male; 59.4%, female) (2005)

Economy

Currency	Egyptian pound; exchange rate 5.78 pounds per U.S. dollar (2005)
GDP Purchasing Power Parity (PPP)	$334.4 billion (2006)
GDP Per Capita	$4,200 (2006 est.)
Labor Force	21.8 million (2006 est.)
Unemployment	10.3% of total population (2006)
Labor Force by Occupation	Services, 51%; agriculture, 32%; industry, 17%
Agricultural Products	Cotton, rice, corn, wheat, beans, fruits, vegetables; cattle, water buffalo, sheep, goats
Industries	Textiles, food processing, tourism, chemicals, hydrocarbons, construction, cement, metals
Exports	$24.22 billion f.o.b. (2006 est.)
Imports	$35.86 billion f.o.b. (2006 est.)

106

Leading Trade Partners	Exports: U.S., 13%; Italy, 9.3%; Spain, 7.7%; Syria, 5.5%; France, 4.9%; Germany, 4.8%; Saudi Arabia, 4.7% (2005); Imports: U.S., 10.6%; Germany, 7%; China, 6.5%; France, 6.3%; Italy, 5.8%; Saudi Arabia, 4.8% (2005)
Export Commodities	Crude oil and petroleum products, cotton, textiles, metal products, chemicals
Import Commodities	Machinery and equipment, foodstuffs, chemicals, wood products, fuels
Transportation	Roadways: 57,396 miles (92,370 kilometers), 46,491 miles (74,820 kilometers) is paved (2004); Railways: 3,146 miles (5,063 kilometers); Airports: 88—72 are paved runways (2006); Waterways: 2,175 miles (3,500 kilometers) *note*: includes Nile River, Lake Nasser, Alexandria-Cairo Waterway, and numerous smaller canals in delta; Suez Canal—121 miles (194 kilometers), including approaches; navigable by oceangoing vessels drawing up to 59 feet (18 meters) (2005)

Government

Country Name	Conventional long form: Arab Republic of Egypt; conventional short form: Egypt; local long form: Jumhuriyat Misral-Arabiyah; local short form: Misr; former: United Arab Republic (with Syria)
Capital City	Cairo
Type of Government	Republic
Chief of State	President Hosni Mubarak (since October 1981)
Independence	February 28, 1922 (from the United Kingdom)
Administrative Divisions	26 governorates (muhafazat, singular—muhafazah)

Communications

TV Stations	98 (1995)
Radio Stations	56 (AM, 42; FM, 14) (2005)
Phones	24,441,000 (including 14,045,000 cell phones) (2005)
Internet Users	5 million (2005)

* Source: *CIA-The World Factbook* (2007)

History at a Glance

3100 B.C.	Upper and Lower Egypt unite under King Menes.
2700–2200	Old Kingdom—during this time the Egyptians build the Great Pyramid and Sphinx.
1570–1090	New Kingdom—the pharaoh Ramses II builds enormous monuments to himself throughout Egypt.
332–30	Ptolemaic (Greek) Period—Alexander the Great rules Egypt.
30 B.C. to A.D. 324	Egypt ruled by the Romans.
A.D. 641	Arabs conquer Egypt and introduce the Islamic religion.
969–1171	The Fatimid Dynasty rules Egypt and moves the capital from Alexandria to Cairo.
1171–1250	Saladin defeats the Fatimids and establishes the Ayyubid Dynasty.
1250–1382	Bahri Mamluk seizes control of Egypt.
1516–1798	Ottoman Turks rule.
1798	Napoleon Bonaparte enters Egypt.
1805–1848	Reign of Muhammad Ali.
1848–1922	Reigns of Ibrahim Abbas I, Said, Ismail, Khedive Tawfiq, Khedive Abbas II, and Ahmed Fu'ad.
1882	British colonization of Egypt begins.
1922	Independence from the United Kingdom; accession of King Fu'ad I.
1928	The Muslim Brotherhood founded in Cairo.
1948	War with Israel.
1952	Gamal Abdel Nasser leads a revolution that ousts King Farouk.
1956–70	Nasser's presidency.
1956	Suez Crisis and war with Great Britain, France, and Israel.
1967	War with Israel.
1971–81	Presidency of Anwar Sadat.
1973	War with Israel.
1979	Camp David Accords lead to peace treaty with Israel; the Sinai Peninsula is returned to Egypt.
1981–88	Presidency of Hosni Mubarak.
1988	Egyptian novelist Naguib Mahfouz becomes first and only Arab to win the Nobel Prize in literature.
1989	Egypt rejoins the Arab League.

1992–1996	Boutros Boutros-Ghali of Egypt serves as UN's secretary-general.
1999	Egyptian scientist Ahmed Zewail becomes the first and only Arab to win the Nobel Prize in the Sciences.
2000	Egypt, Lebanon, and Syria agree to a billion-dollar oil pipeline deal.
2004	Funeral of erstwhile Palestine leader Yasser Arafat takes place in Cairo.
2005	President Hosni Mubarak reelected for his fifth consecutive term.

Bibliography

Anderson, Ewan W. *The Middle East: Geography and Geopolitics*. London: Routledge, 2000.

Beaumont, Peter, Gerald H. Blake, and Malcolm J. Wagstaff. *The Middle East: A Geographical Study* (Second Edition). New York: Halsted, 1988.

Bill, James A., and Robert Springbord. *Politics in the Middle East* (Third Edition). Glenview, Ill.: Scott, Foresman/Little, Brown, 1990.

Bowen, Donna Lee, and Evelyn A Early. *Everyday Life in the Muslim Middle East*. Bloomington: Indiana University Press, 1993.

Breasted, James Henry. *A History of Egypt*. New York: Bantam, 1964.

Fahmy, Khaled. *All the Pashas Men: Mehmed Ali His Army and the Making of Modern Egypt*. Cairo: American University in Cairo Press, 2002.

Gelvin, James L. *The Modern Middle East: A History*. New York: Oxford, 2004.

Goldschmidt, Arthur. *A Concise History of the Middle East*. Boulder, Colo.: Westview Press, 1991.

——. *Modern Egypt: The Formation of a Nation-State*. Boulder, Colo.: Westview Press, 2004.

Goodman, Steven M., and Peter L. Meininger eds. *The Birds of Egypt*. Oxford: Oxford University Press, 1989.

Held, Colbert C. *Middle East Patterns: Places, People and Politics* (Third Edition). Boulder, Colo.: Westview Press, 2000.

Lippman, Thomas W. *Egypt After Nasser*. New York: Paragon House, 1989.

Rawlinson, George, trans. *Herodotus Histories*. Ware, Hertfordshire: Wordsworth, 1996.

Waterbury, John. *Hydropolitics of the Nile Valley*. Syracuse, N.Y.: Syracuse University Press, 1979.

Youssef, Hisham, and John Rodenbeck, eds. *Insight Guides: Egypt*. Boston: Houghton Mifflin, 1997.

Books

Asante, Molefi Kete. *Cultures and Customs of Egypt.* Westport, Conn.: Greenwood Press, 2002.

Christensen, Wendy. *Empire of Ancient Egypt.* New York: Facts On File, 2004.

Goldschmidt, Arthur Jr. *A Brief History of Egypt.* New York: Facts On File, 2007.

Hunt, Norman Bancroft. *Living in Ancient Egypt.* New York: Facts On File, 2007.

Shaw, Ian. *Exploring Ancient Egypt.* New York: Oxford University Press, 2003.

Web sites

CIA-The World Factbook: Egypt
http://www.cia.gov/cia/publications/factbook/index.html

Geography and Agriculture of Egypt
http://www.mnsu.edu/emuseum/prehistory/egypt/dailylife/ geographyandagriculture.html

The Nile and Ancient Egypt
http://nefertiti.iwebland.com/geography/nile.htm

Egypt Fun Guide
http://www.seaworld.org/fun%2Dzone/fun%2Dguides/egypt/index.htm

U.S. Department of State Background Notes: Egypt
http://www.state.gov/r/pa/ei/bgn/5309.htm

Picture Credits

Index

Index

About the Contributors

JOSEPH J. HOBBS is professor of geography at the University of Missouri–Columbia. He has spent many years in Egypt, studying Egyptology and Arabic and doing field research on the natural environments and cultures of the Bedouin peoples of the Eastern Desert and the Sinai Peninsula. His major books on Egypt are *Bedouin Life in the Egyptian Wilderness* and *Mount Sinai* (both University of Texas Press).

ASWIN SUBANTHORE is a geographer, currently pursuing his doctoral degree and serving as a teaching associate at Oklahoma State University. A native of Chennai, India, his thematic research interest is in cultural geography, with regional interests in South Asia, West Asia, and the Arab world.

CHARLES F. GRITZNER is distinguished professor of geography at South Dakota State University. He is now in his fifth decade of college teaching and research. Much of his career work has focused on geographic education. He has served as both president and executive director of the National Council for Geographic Education and has received the Council's George J. Miller Award for Distinguished Service.